Do-it-yourself

Motoring
Law

Felicity Mileham

LAW PACK™
GUIDE

Published by
Law Pack Publishing Limited
10-16 Cole Street
London SE1 4YH
Internet www.lawpack.co.uk

Motoring Law Guide

© Law Pack Publishing Limited 1999
ISBN: 1-898217-51-3
All rights reserved.

Printed in the United Kingdom

Important facts

This **Law Pack Guide** contains information and advice on the law as it applies to the motorist and his car, and on motoring-related offences in the civil and criminal justice systems of England & Wales. Court procedures of Scotland and Northern Ireland are not included, but many of the principles of the law discussed in this Guide apply throughout the United Kingdom.

The information it contains has been carefully compiled from professional sources, but its accuracy is not guaranteed, as laws and regulations may change or be subject to differing interpretations. The law is stated as at 1st January 1999.

Neither this nor any other publication can take the place of a solicitor on important legal matters. As with any legal matter, common sense should determine whether you need the assistance of a solicitor rather than relying solely on the information and forms in this **Law Pack Guide**.

Table of contents

How to use this Law Pack Guide

This Law Pack Guide can help you achieve important legal objectives conveniently, efficiently and economically. Remember that it is important for you to use this Guide properly if you are to avoid later difficulties.

Step-by-step instructions for using this Guide:

1. Read this Guide carefully. If after thorough examination you decide that your requirements are not met by this Law Pack Guide, or you do not feel confident about writing your own documents, consult a solicitor.

2. Each chapter deals with a separate area of motoring law. An overview of the legislation is given, together with tips, practical advice, example scenarios and sample documents. There are tables summarising useful data, such as penalties for various motoring offences.

3. Also included are details on how the civil and criminal justice systems work. Police and Court procedures are described, with example documents to help you prepare your own where necessary.

4. Always use pen or type on legal documents; never use a pencil.

5. Do not cross out or erase anything on your final documents.

6. Always keep legal documents in a safe place and in a location known to your next of kin or solicitor.

Introduction

Motoring law affects us all. This is particularly so for drivers and motorcycle owners, but it is also true for pedestrians and other road users. Every time we get into a car there are implications in criminal law (the panoply of road traffic offences) and in civil law (our duty to take care for the safety of other road users). Buying a vehicle involves us in the law of contract amongst other things and driving abroad brings us into contact with the law of foreign countries.

This Guide is intended to provide an overview of each of these things and other areas of motoring law for the motorist. The emphasis is on practical advice, rather than than in-depth analysis of the substantive law. Checklists, diagrams and tables are included to help you analyse your situation. The Guide also outlines the Court procedures to help you when you are being prosecuted, sued or when you are suing someone else.Where matters are too serious or complex to be dealt with by a general Guide such as this you are warned to take legal advice. However, with the help of this Guide it is hoped you will become aware of your rights as a motorist, and will be able to deal with the Courts with confidence. Happy motoring!

Felicity Mileham

Mitre Court Chambers

Chapter

Dealing with the garage

When you buy a car (or bicycle or motorbike) or have one repaired the deal between you and the seller or garage is governed by the law of contract, a branch of the civil law. Of course, if a seller has acted in bad faith or unlawfully there may also be other legal consequences (e.g. a crime may have been committed, or Trading Standards infringed). This chapter, however, concentrates on how to avoid the pitfalls when dealing with the garage or private seller, and describes what you can claim for if things have gone wrong. Whilst the chapter refers to buying cars the principles apply also to the purchase of bicycles, motor bicycles and other vehicles.

Buying a car

New

If you are buying a new car you will be dealing with a dealer (i.e. a person or company whose business it is to sell cars), and the chances are that the contract will be a written one, and probably will include a warranty, and package of other benefits.

Used

You might purchase a used car from a dealer or from a private individual, in which case the contract may be written, oral or both. The protection given to you by the law is different in each of these cases and are discussed below. However, the fundamental principle remains that you can sue the seller if there has been 'breach of contract' or if he/she has 'misrepresented' a material fact which had induced you to buy the car. Misrepresentation is dealt with separately below. Finally, a word of warning, this Guide deals solely with the legal position in dealing with the garage, only mentioning in passing how you can safeguard yourself against buying an expensive and troublesome dud. There are many specialist books available which give advice on what mechanical defects and 'tricks of the trade' to look out for, as well as market prices guidelines. These should be referred to in order to avoid ever having to call upon the law!

Breach of contract – buying from a dealer

As long as you are a private consumer the Sale of Goods Act 1979 (as amended) offers you some protection. This is because the Act demands that cars (or bicycles and motor bicycles) sold to private consumers by dealers must be of 'satisfactory quality'. This is a question of fact, and the Courts will take account of the price paid, the make, age and model, and any other relevant factors. The Act also requires that a car sold to a consumer must also be reasonably fit for a purpose made known to the seller by the buyer. Usually the buyer will by implication require a car that can be driven along a road for a reasonable mileage and period after the purchase. Thus if the car becomes undriveable shortly after it was bought you may have a claim against the seller. If you told the garage that you wanted the car for a specific purpose and the car turns out to be unfit for that purpose you may also have a claim.

Warning!

If the seller draws your attention to a defect before you buy the car, you will not be able to complain about it at a later date. Similarly, if you have had a chance to examine the car before purchasing and fail to spot or decide to ignore a defect should have been apparent to you, you will not be able to sue in respect of that defect. This might occur, for example, if the door handle was broken.

Quite simply, you get what you pay for. What may be an unacceptable fault in a new or nearly-new car may not be (legally) unacceptable in an elderly car of large mileage which you bought at a comparatively low market price. The older the car the more problems it is likely to get and the courts will take this into account.

Breach of contract – buying from a private seller

When you buy a car (bicycle or motorbike) from someone who does not sell cars for a living there is no protection from the Sale of Goods Act. Basically, 'buyer beware!'. This means it is up to you to ensure that there are no defects before you buy. You are unlikely to be able to sue the seller for defects that become apparent after the sale, and the best advice is to ensure that you know as much as possible about the vehicle, its condition and history, before you hand over any money.

Misrepresentation

If the vehicle does not match up to the description or promises made by the seller (either a dealer or an individual) before the deal was struck, you may be able to claim for 'misrepresentation', (whether or not the seller acted in good faith). Note also that only statements of fact, rather than opinions or law can amount to a misrepresentation.

If there has been a misrepresentation you are entitled either to your money back (and return of the car to the previous owner), or to a sum representing the difference in value between the value of the car you contracted to buy and the value of the car that you actually got. If you wish to return the car and obtain a refund of the money you paid out you <u>must act quickly</u>. Often where the purchaser has delayed returning the car (or telling the seller to come and pick it up), or a long time has passed since the contract was formed the Courts will simply award the buyer damages (in practice. a smaller sum than the purchase price). Of course, your other option is to report the matter to Trading Standards who may prosecute the seller. A successful conviction of the seller may result in you being awarded compensation by the Court.

Example:

Miss A tells Mr B that the car she wants to sell has a mileage of 60,000. Mr B likes the car and partly relying on the fact that the car only has 60,000 on the clock agrees to buy. It transpires that the car has been 'clocked 'and the true mileage is 120,000 miles. Mr B has a claim for misrepresentation against Miss A.

How to make a claim

The first step is to offer the seller, whether a company, individual car dealer or private person, the opportunity of putting matters right. If there has been a substantial breach of contract (e.g. major repairs or replacement of parts needed) or if there has been a misrepresentation, and you do not want to keep the car, write to the seller at once stating that you want to return the car. You should tell him or her to arrange to pick up the car, and do not use it further. If you paid for the car in instalments do not pay any more. Instead ask the seller to return the money you have already paid to him. If this does not work send a 'letter before action' which asks him to return your money and collect the car within a certain time and warns him that if he does not do so you will take him to Court.

If you are happy to keep the car, but want the defects put right (breach of contract), or a refund to reflect the difference in value of the car you contracted to buy and the car you were sold (misrepresentation) write to the seller and outline what has gone wrong. It is often helpful (and persuasive!) to include a photocopy of any documents that support your claim. This might be in the form of an engineer's report, or garage estimate. If you get nowhere the next step is a 'letter before action' asking him to comply with your requests within a specified time-limit or be taken to court.

Going to the County Court

For general information about taking someone to court see Chapter 2. Firstly you must 'issue proceedings' by filling in a form which gives details of the parties, sets out your claim, and asks for the court to grant a remedy (e.g. compensation). This form will be filed at Court on payment of the appropriate fee. If the seller is going to fight the claim he will fill in a 'Defence' form and send that to the Court. The Court then will lay down a strict timetable for the preparations for trial. If the money claimed is less than £3000 the action will be set down for 'Arbitration' (Small Claims Court).

One important thing to remember is to ensure you sue the correct person. If the seller was an individual they can be named as defendant, e.g. John Smith. If you purchased your car from a company the company should be sued, e.g. 'Cars Are Us Limited'. If you are in any doubt as to whom you should be suing obtain advice at a Citizens' Advice Bureau or Law Centre. It is very important to get it right, not least because your case may get thrown out before it gets anywhere, and you will incur further legal costs if you want to begin again.

Remember to collect evidence to support your claim. By the time you are considering going to Court you may have already obtained an expert's report on what is wrong with the car. You will also need estimates on how much your car is worth now as a result of the defect or misrepresentation, and/or estimates on how much it will cost to repair. The Court will also want to see all the contractual documents. Photographs of the car and the defects may help your case.

The following page provides an example 'Particulars of Claim', which is the part of the form outlining your case. Remember to

a) name the parties

b) identify the contract details (who, what and when)

c) specify the breach or misrepresentation

d) state the expenses you have incurred or will incur

e) ask the Court for compensation ('damages') or a refund

f) ask for interest pursuant to the County Courts Act 1984 (section 69)

Example Particulars of Claim

PARTICULARS OF CLAIM

1. The Defendant was at all material times a company selling motor cars in the course of its business.

2. On or about the 20th October 1998 by a written agreement the Plaintiff agreed to buy an Austin Maestro Registration Number [   ] from the Defendant for £500 ('the contract').

3. It was an implied term of the contract that the motor vehicle was of satisfactory quality.

4. On the 21st of October whilst the Plaintiff was driving the car down the High Street, Anytown, it broke down and could not be driven until repaired by a mechanic.

5. In breach of contract the car was not of satisfactory quality in that:

PARTICULARS OF BREACH

5.1 [list the defects]

6. By reason of the above matters the Plaintiff has suffered loss and damage

PARTICULARS OF DAMAGE

(1) cost of repair   £250.00

7. The Plaintiff claims interest pursuant to section 69 of the County Courts Act 1984 for such a period and at such a rate as the Court thinks fit.

AND the Plaintiff claims;

(1) damages

(2) interest as aforesaid pursuant to section 69 of the County Courts Act 1984.

Served...[date] by [name]

Remember, the Court will provide you with the necessary forms and some guidance. For further details on making civil claims see Chapter 3. If in any doubt contact your Citizens Advice Bureau, Law Centre or solicitor, for an assessment of the strength of your case and practical advice.

Miscellaneous information

Stolen vehicles

If you buy a vehicle that subsequently turns out to have been stolen you have no rights over it as it still belongs to the original owner (or the insurance company). Your only claim is against the person who sold it to you, which may be difficult in practice. If the seller is convicted of theft, or a related crime in respect of the car, the Court may award you compensation, but this is unlikely to get you all your money back. To guard against this unfortunate position it is sensible to do a check on the vehicle before you buy. Equifax is an organisation which will search a database to see if the car you intend to buy has been reported stolen, 'written off' by the insurers or still subject to a Hire Purchase agreement. Equifax can be contacted on telephone 01722 413434. You will be charged a fee for this service, currently £31.00.

'Ringing' and 'clocking'.

Unscrupulous sellers may have given a stolen car a new identity by swapping the Registration plates, obtaining replacement paperwork from the DVLA and re-engraving the chassis and engine numbers. This is known as 'ringing'. To lessen the risk of buying such a car obtain an Equifax check by telephone. This may reveal the car to be a write off or stolen. Otherwise keep an eye out for physical marks of an altered identity. 'Clocking' is the illegal practice of winding back the mileometer to show a lesser mileage. There may be visible signs of the fascia being forced (scratched plastic,) or signals that the car may have been much more used than the mileage suggests (i.e. a higher than expected degree of wear and tear).

Having your car repaired at a garage

When you take the car into the garage both you and the garage have contractual responsibilities to fulfill. The work you have asked them to do must be done with 'reasonable skill and care', however they may refuse to release your car until the fees are paid. This is known as 'exercising a lien' over your property, and is lawful. Of course, most defects are not immediately apparent and will only be detected after you have paid the garage on removing your car, so in practice this situation will rarely arise. If you are unhappy about the service you have been given you should pay the sum required, and obtain a report from another engineer analysing the condition of the car and stating whether the service provided was negligent or not. If you are successful in proving the garage did not provide the appropriate standard of service the cost of such an expert report, together with other legal costs will normally be recoverable.

Buying a used car: a checklist

- Read all the vehicle documents very closely
- Read any contractual document or warranty carefully
- Obtain as many details about the seller as you can
- Look out for signs that the car has been clocked
- Run an Equifax check
- Obtain an independent report on the car if you are at all unsure of its condition
- If you part with any money, insist on a receipt

Chapter

Accidents and civil claims

You may find yourself involved with the civil law if you have an accident in your car. If:

1. Your car is damaged by someone else, or you suffer physical injury in the accident, the driver at fault can be asked to pay you compensation the civil Courts. This is known as a claim' for 'damages'.

2. You damage someone else's car or cause someone physical injury in an accident you may be liable to pay compensation or damages to the 'victim'.

3. Both drivers claim the other is at fault both may claim compensation. This takes the form of a 'claim' and 'counterclaim' for 'damages'. The Court must them decide who should pay what to whom.

Civil law exists alongside criminal law. The civil law provides for the party at fault to compensate the innocent party for loss and damage (i.e. the cost of repairing a damaged vehicle, or the value of a 'written off' one). Compensation for personal injury can also be ordered by a court; this will include sums for incidental expenses past and future and an amount representing 'pain, suffering and loss of amenity'.

The Criminal Justice System exists for the state to punish offenders. The police and the Crown Prosecution Service are responsible for gathering the evidence and prosecuting the offender.

In some circumstances there will be overlap on civil and criminal law. For example a driver involved in an accident may find himself prosecuted for careless driving (criminal proceedings) in the local Magistrates or Crown Court, and also be taken to the County Court or High Court by the other driver in a civil action for 'negligence'.

The purpose of this chapter is to describe:

- ■ What to do after an accident

- ■ Who is to bear responsibility for paying for damage / personal injury

- ■ When to get a lawyer

- ■ How to claim against someone in the Small Claims Court; or what to do if someone brings a claim against you.

But first a word about insurance...

Insurance

Insurance is compulsory for the motorist. By law, everyone who drives a car, or an owner of a car who allows someone else to drive him or her in that car must have a valid insurance policy covering at least 'third party risks'. Many people have 'comprehensive cover' instead. It is an offence to use or drive the car, or to allow yourself to be driven in your car without valid insurance.

Third party cover

This means the insurance company will pay out compensation for damage caused to passengers or other road users caused by your negligent driving.

Comprehensive insurance cover

This usually means in addition to third party cover the insurance company will pay out for damage to your own car and personal injury to yourself. The policy may also cover your legal expenses, compensation for theft and providing a courtesy car. Remember, however, insurance policies vary and you must check to see exactly what you are covered for. Conditions may also apply. Common examples are cover limited to 'named drivers', cover only for social and domestic use of the car; and no cover for use on private land. If you drive whilst disqualified the insurance is automatically invalidated – you are thus committing two offences.

The Motor Insurers' Bureau (MIB)

All the motor insurance companies belong to this organisation. It pays compensation up to a maximum of £250,000 where:

a)   You successfully sue a driver who had no insurance cover and cannot otherwise afford to pay the damages awarded to you.

b)   In a 'hit and run' accident where the guilty driver cannot be traced and therefore cannot be taken to court. This is dealt with under the 'Untraced Drivers Agreement'. The Bureau investigates your claim and the circumstances of the incident and may make an award. You can appeal against their decision.

Minor accidents

Is someone at fault?

Every driver must drive with the 'ordinary care and skill' of a competent qualified driver. If a driver falls below this standard and causes damage or injury to another road user or nearby property he or she will be 'liable in negligence'. This section deals with minor traffic accidents. If you are involved in a serious accident (i.e. someone is seriously injured, property is badly damaged or the emergency services are involved) it is wise to seek legal advice. Of course, if you are injured you may not be able to deal with the immediate aftermath of the accident.

Most accidents occur between two or more vehicles (cars, motorcycles buses, etc). However, a motorist may be involved in an accident with a pedestrian, roadside property, animals or parked vehicles. Whatever the situation, the motorist is expected to exercise the ordinary skill and care of a competent and qualified driver.

Common examples of liability

■ Veering or pulling out into the path of lane of another vehicle without adequate warning.

■ Driving too fast for the road conditions and not being able to stop in time to avoid collision.

■ Failing to keep a satisfactory look out for vehicles or other hazards.

Whether a driver will be found by a Court to have fallen below the standard of driving expected of him depends on the circumstances of the case. Failure to observe the recommendations of the Highway Code can be used to show a driver was negligent. On the other hand, showing the Court that the recommendations of the Highway Code were followed help to show the driver was not negligent.

Accidents - what to do if you have one

Duty to exchange details

Do not leave the scene of the accident immediately. You must stop for a reasonable length of time to allow any interested party (the other driver or the owner of property or an animal damaged or injured), or a policeman to take your details.

Failure to (a) stop and/or (b) to give details if asked is an offence and carries a maximum penalty of 6 months imprisonment; a fine of up to

£5000; 5-10 penalty points or discretionary disqualification from driving.

The details required are:

a)   your name and address;

b)   if you were driving someone else's vehicle, the name and address of the owner;

c)   the identification marks of the vehicle (including the registration number);

d)   if someone was injured, you must produce your insurance certificate; see 'Reporting the accident' below if you cannot produce it at this time .

Do not admit liability

It is sensible not to admit liability at the scene of the accident. You may be upset or angry, and questions of liability can be dealt with later. Even if you think you may have been at fault later evidence might show that the other driver contributed to the accident, and this may affect the amount of compensation you or your insurers will have to pay. If any conversation does pass about who was at fault make a note of what was said by whom as soon as possible afterwards.

Take witnesses' details

If there is anyone who saw the accident and is prepared to be a witness or give a statement take their name and address and tell them that you will contact them. If your insurance company decides to conduct your case it may take on the responsibility of contacting witnesses for you (often through solicitors). If you are conducting your own case you will have to notify them yourself of any Court dates. Note that travel costs and something towards lost earnings in respect of attending at Court are recoverable in the Small Claims Courts for witness if you win.

Remember that the evidence of independent witnesses is stronger that non-independent witnesses, and that eyewitnesses are more helpful than people who did not actually see the accident happen.

Example:

You are the driver of a red car and are involved in a collision with a blue car. Your passenger is WITNESS A: the driver of a yellow car is WITNESS B: and a pedestrian WITNESS C:

WITNESS A: *"I was the passenger in the red car which was being driven by my best friend along the High Street at 25 mph. Suddenly the blue car shot out of a side road called Wellgreen Avenue. My friend did not have time to brake and the two cars collided."*

This witness is not independent as he knows the driver of the red car, however, he saw the accident happen and can give useful information.

WITNESS B: *"I was parked at a parking meter on the High Street 50 yards away from the junction of the High Street and Wellgreen Avenue. Suddenly I saw a red car coming towards me on the other side of the road at about 30 mph. Then I saw the blue car drive quickly out of Wellgreen Avenue directly into the path of the red car which did not have time to avoid the collision. The red car was shunted onto the other side of the road."*

This witness is independent and an eyewitness. Her evidence is extremely helpful.

WITNESS C: *" I was looking in a shop window on the High Street near the junction with Wellgreen Avenue. Out of the corner of my eye I noticed a red car drive along the High Street towards the junction. Seconds later I heard the screech of brakes and then a loud bang. I turned round and saw that the red car had collided with a blue car. When I got closer I saw that the blue car had shunted the red car right onto the other side of the High Street."*

This independent witness did not see the accident occur, and therefore cannot give direct evidence as to which driver was at fault. However he can testify to the following facts: (i) which cars were involved, (ii) that one car at least tried to brake to avoid the accident, (iii) the position of the cars after the collision. All these factors may help a Court decide who was to blame.

Don't forget that you can be a witness, too!

Reporting the accident

Do you need to report the accident?

Unless you have exchanged details with anyone who had reasonable cause to ask you, e.g. the owner of damaged property or a police constable attending at the scene, you <u>must</u> report the accident if:

a)   any person (other than you) was injured, including passengers in your car and/or

b)   a domestic or farm animal was injured of killed (cats not included) and/or

c)   property (other than your car) was damaged: this includes buildings/plants/trees adjoining the road, street furniture such as bollards and lamp posts, or another vehicle.

How and when must I report?

You must report the accident in person (a telephone call will not do) either to a police officer or at a police station at the earliest practicable time within 24 hours of the accident. Failure to do so is an offence. The maximum sentence is 6 months imprisonment and/or a fine up to £5000. Disqualification from driving is available, and the magistrates can endorse your licence with 5-10 points.

Note that if someone was injured and you did not produce your insurance certificate on request at the scene you must show it to the police

i)   either when you report the accident or

ii)   within 7 days of reporting the accident to the police

Failure to produce your insurance certificate is an offence which is punishable by a fine up to £1000.

Making notes and keeping records

Your insurers may provide you with a claim form to fill in which asks for all the following information. However, it is a good idea to do the following as soon as practicable after the accident;

a)   Draw a plan of the site 'before' and 'after' the accident from memory. It should show the position of the parties involved, direction of the vehicles; road names and numbers, and any relevant road markings (see example on next page).

Example 'before' and 'after' accident diagram

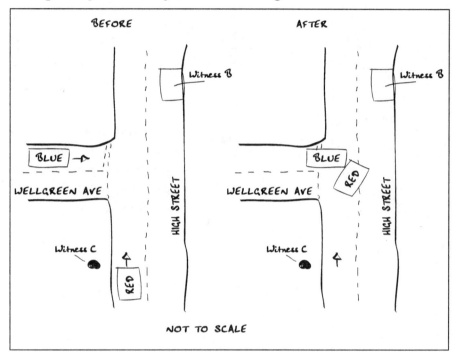

Highlight

If possible, take photographs of the site to show the layout of the road clearly

b) Make a note of your version of the accident. Remember to describe the following:

- the road conditions (weather/light/weight of traffic)
- speed limits on the road in question
- how you approached the site of the accident and at what speed
- how the other vehicle approached the site and its speed
- any warning from either driver (e.g. use of indicators, horn or lights)
- the nature and extent of the damage to both vehicles, and any injuries.
- anything said by either of the parties, or a witness.

c) If possible, take photographs of the site to show the layout of the road clearly. It is helpful also to make a record of where each photograph was taken from on a diagram (see example on next page).

Example diagram showing position of photographs

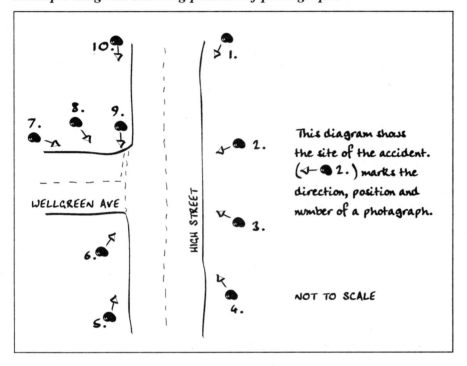

d)   Take photographs of the damaged vehicle or property.

e)   If you have been injured keep a diary of the persistence of your symptoms, any attendance at medical appointments or any treatment you receive.

f)   Make a list of damaged property (e.g. spectacles, clothes, goods carried in the vehicle that have become damaged) and its value.

Paperwork

Keep records of everything! Make copies of any letters you write or forms you fill in respecting the accident. Keep all your receipts (remember particularly the insurance excess receipt that you may have to pay to the garage when your car is repaired). As for repair estimates, the insurance company may deal with this for you or they may require you to obtain your own estimates. It is sensible to obtain at least two estimates from reputable garages.

Report the claim to your insurer

This may be a condition of your insurance contract, even if you do not intend to make a claim against your own insurers, or to ask your insurers to claim against the other driver. The insurer will tell you what cover you have.

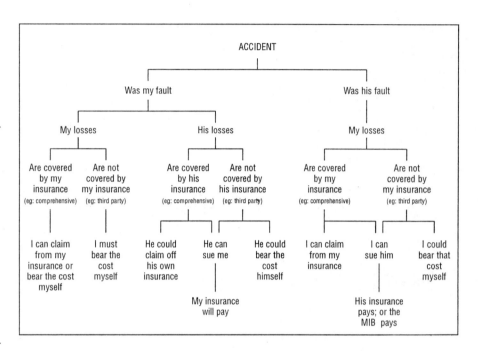

Highlight

Remember, it is not worth going to Court merely to get an apology. The most you can expect is compensation. If the other driver or his insurers make a sensible offer it is wise to accept it

The chart above shows in what circumstances insurance claims can be made, and whose insurance company will have to pay for compensation. Remember, it is not worth going to Court merely to get an apology. The most you can expect is compensation. If the other driver or his insurers make a sensible offer it is wise to accept it.

Do you need a lawyer?

The majority of accidents are dealt with by insurers. However, the rest of this chapter explains how to deal with the civil Courts in the event that you:

1) want to fight your case yourself;

2) want to claim back the excess and any other sums not reimbursed by the insurer;

3) simply want to be well-informed, for future eventualities.

If your insurers are conducting your claim they may instruct a lawyer on your behalf. This will happen if the claim is to be fought in the County or High Court. Some insurance policies will offer cover for legal expenses in respect of uninsured losses (e.g. to allow you to recover the 'policy excess' you had to pay from the other driver). However, if you are not receiving legal help from your insurers you must decide, in the early stages after an accident and if the claim is going to the Small Claims Court where the claim for compensation is currently up to £3,000 (or £1,000 if there is a claim in respect of a personal injury); whether or not to seek legal help.

A solicitor can:

a) give advice on liability (i.e. who was legally at fault, or if there is a defence)

b) give advice on how much you can expect (or expect to pay) in compensation; this is particularly important if there is a claim for personal injury – they are difficult to calculate

c) help you decide whether to make or accept an offer of settlement (an 'out of Court' settlement) and negotiate on your behalf

d) represent you in court, or instruct a barrister to do so.

The Small Claims Court is part of the County Court. The procedure at the hearing is designed for the non-lawyer (although, if you wish, you can have a solicitor of barrister to represent you). Note that Legal Aid is not available for Small Claims arbitrations. Nor can you recover your legal costs from the losing party in the Small Claims Court. This means that you must pay the lawyer's fee yourself. Check with your insurers as you may have cover for this sort of expense. In other civil Courts the Court will often order the 'loser' to pay the winner of a claim or counterclaim legal costs as well as compensation. This makes litigation very expensive!

A good place to start is to contact your local Citizens Advice Bureau. This service is free and they will be able to:

a) help you decide whether to seek advice from a solicitor or law centre

b) help you fill in forms relating to your claim or defence

c) give you further information about what to do next.

Negotiated settlements

If your insurance company is dealing with your case it may make or accept an offer on your behalf. This will result in the ending of Court proceedings and, usually, the payment of compensation by one party to the other. The insurance company will make a decision whether to settle after considering the evidence you have supplied in your claim form, anything said about liability by the other driver or his insurer, and other commercial matters.

If, however, you decide to bypass your insurance company by not making a claim you may have to consider if it is in your interests to make or accept an offer of settlement. First consider whether you need a lawyer's help. This is particularly important if the claim is a large one, or there is a claim for personal injury, as the rules about how much compensation is recoverable are complex, and medical reports may have to be evaluated.

Once having decided to settle your case you must first decide what sum of money you should offer (or accept). The following points are important whether you are a defendant who is offering to pay the plaintiff, or a plaintiff considering accepting the defendant's offer.

How much should the offer be?

The starting point is how much the injured party can expect to recover in a court of law:

1) The cost of repairing a car or other property damaged in the accident. Where property would cost more to repair than its actual worth it is called 'beyond economic repair' or a 'write-off' and the write-off value is recoverable instead.

2) The costs incurred reasonably as a result of damage to property or injury

   e.g. the cost of using public transport whilst a car was off the road or being repaired,

   e.g. the cost of doctors' report fees, emergency treatment fees and prescriptions in a case of personal injury.

3) A sum representing loss of earnings and 'pain suffering and loss of amenity' in respect of a personal injury. The sum tries to represent compensation for the pain caused by the injury and the effect it has on your life. For example, an injury which causes a great deal of pain and requires long-term treatment, restricts the sufferer's ability to do the housework and prevents her from continuing her hobby of competitive windsurfing will require more compensation than an injury that needs minimal treatment, heals quickly, and does not stop the sufferer from working and living as normal after some initial discomfort. To establish this you will need legal advice, as the Courts look to compensation paid out in previous cases. All but the most minor of injuries are dealt with by the County Court, rather than by Small Claims Arbitration (i.e. Small Claims Court).

The next thing to consider are the factors that invariably reduce the starting figure:

1) *The risks of litigation.*

   If the case does not settle, the parties will have their evidence tested in Court or Arbitration. There is always a chance that you might not prove your case or defence. The weaker a party's evidence the riskier the litigation. This is particularly so in road traffic cases where there are independent witnesses and one driver's word is against the other's. It may be simpler and cheaper to settle before the case comes to Court!

2)   *Compensation will be paid sooner.*

All Court cases, even straightforward Small Claims cases, take time. Even if the Court orders compensation there may be further delay of 'enforcing judgment' (i.e. actually obtaining payment of the damages).

3)   *Convenience.*

While some people will not be worried by the prospect of going to Court or Arbitration, many people will be nervous of having to give evidence, especially under cross examination. Additionally, the inevitable delay of Court proceedings means that the prospect of going to Court may be hanging over one for a period of months. Settlement shortens the delay and avoids the case having to come before the Court.

4)   *It's not worth having your day in Court.*

Remember, it is not worth going to Court just to get an apology. If the offer is sensible, accept it. If you think that you will be ordered to pay compensation by a Court, make a realistic offer at this stage.

Taking your case to Court

This section describes the steps you need to take to bring your case in the Small Claims Court. The Small Claims Court is designed to be used by non-lawyers, where the money claimed is (at present) £3,000 or less; or £1,000 where your claim includes a claim of compensation for injury. For a more in-depth coverage of this subject refer to the **Law Pack** *Small Claims Guide*.

Who should you sue?

The person who is the 'innocent' party (the plaintiff) sues the person or persons who caused his loss or damage (the defendant). Therefore where the 'innocent' driver does not own the car he was driving the owner will have suffered the loss, not the driver. In that case it is the owner that should sue.

Example

A son is driving his mother's car when he is involved in an accident. He believes the other driver was to blame. In the accident the car sustained £500 worth of damage. His mother should sue the negligent driver. She will need to give evidence that she owns the car and that £500 worth of damage was caused. Her son should be called as a witness to tell the court how the accident happened.

Where more than one person suffers loss in the accident each can sue; they will be co-plaintiffs.

Example

A son is driving his mother's car when he is involved in an accident. The car suffers £500 worth of damage and the son's computer, which was in the boot at the time will cost £800 to repair. The son also suffered a mild whiplash neck injury. In this case both the mother and son should sue as co-plaintiffs as they both have separate claims from the defendant arising from the same accident.

Either innocent party can start the ball rolling and the other can be 'joined', or both can start actions separately which are then consolidated and heard together. For further information consult a law centre, Citizens' Advice Bureau or solicitor. It is much easier however for plaintiffs to begin an action together simply by filling in the forms in their joint names and clearly identifying the damages claimed by each.

In the same way as there can be one or more plaintiff, there can be one or more defendant. At the hearing the court may decide how blame should be apportioned between them (e.g. 50:50). If the 'guilty' party was driving in the course of his or her employment, for example a bus driver, you should sue the employer. A company can be named as a defendant and will usually be liable for the negligence of its employees. Note that this does not include self-employed people or sub-contractors.

Letter before action

Before suing someone it is considered good practice to send a 'letter before action'. This warns the other motorist that you hold him responsible for the accident and that he has one last chance to pay for the damage he caused before being sued. An example letter is provided on the following page.

Example letter before action

Miss Joanna Smith
The Cottage
Anytown
County
AB1 2CD

12 January 1999

Dear Mr Green

Accident at High Street, Anytown at 3pm on 3 January 1999

As a result of this accident I [suffered loss and damage to my car/personal property][had to pay a policy excess of £100 to my motor insurers][suffered personal injury, namely bruising to my right elbow].

Having considered the circumstances of the accident I believe you were to blame for the accident. You were negligent in that you amongst other things [drove too fast/emerged from a side road without giving due priority to vehicles on the main road/failed to keep a proper lookout/failed to avoid collision].

If you accept liability please notify me in writing within [14 days] of the date of this letter [enclosing a cheque for £xxx made payable to Miss Joanna Smith]. If I do not receive your notification [and payment] within [14 days] I will issue proceedings in the Anytown County Court.

Yours sincerely

Joanna Smith

Joanna Smith

Remember to keep a copy of any letter that you send or receive. If your letter before action produces a response all well and good. If you asked for a specified sum in the letter but do not receive any or the full amount claimed you can sue for the remainder (but see 'Negotiated Settlements' above on accepting offers of settlement – if the amount offered is not much less than the sum you asked for it may be worth accepting). If the other motorist simply accepted liability your options are:

    a)   agree between you the amount that the defendant will pay you in 'full and final settlement' of your claim

    b)   ask the Court to assess how much the defendant should pay to you (called 'asking for assessment of damages').

For guidelines as to what sum you can claim see 'How much should the offer be?'

If you have no reply the next stage is to 'issue proceedings'.

Issuing proceedings

The plaintiff must:

    1)   File a County Court Summons (Form N1 or N2)

    2)   Give 'particulars' of his claim.

You can obtain blank forms from the County Court. If you can calculate exactly how much money the 'defendant' should pay you use Form N1. This would be the case where the cost of repairing the car or damaged goods is known, or you are claiming for the amount of the policy excess. On the other hand there may be situations where you must ask the court to arrive at a figure in which case you need to fill in Form N2.

N1 and N2 contain guidelines to help you fill in the information. Whichever type of form you complete you will need to send two copies to the Court (one for the Court file and one for the Court to send on to the defendant). You will need to retain a third copy for your own records.

Particulars of the plaintiff's claim

The plaintiff sets out the details of his allegations either on the Form or on a separate sheet of paper entitled 'Particulars of Claim' (in this case fill in the box on the form: 'See Particulars of Claim'). Example 'particulars of claims' are provided on page 35 and 37. Adapt them to fit circumstances of the case.

The defendant's response

The Court will send the plaintiff's claim to the defendant, along with the forms to fill in which the defendant can

a)   admit part or all of the claim

b)   deny the claim

c)   assert a counterclaim

If the defendant does not reply to the Court the plaintiff can apply for judgment. Read the forms carefully! They explain what you should do. Court staff, although they will not give legal advice, can answer questions on the procedure.

Where the defendant wants to defend the claim he should send a 'Defence' on a separate sheet of paper with the reply form together with a copy for the plaintiff. If he wants to counterclaim he should send a 'Defence and Counterclaim' with the forms. This enables him to set out his allegations in full, rather than being confined to the small boxes on the form.

For a specimen 'Defence' and a specimen 'Defence and Counterclaim' see pages 36 and 38.

Preparing for the Hearing

Directions of the Court

The Court will send you a notice that you should serve the documents you intend to rely on in the hearing, whether you are plaintiff or defendant, on the other party. This means sending a copy of each letter, receipt, report and duplicates of photographs you intend to use, to the other party. You should comply with this order as it will help to clarify the position of the parties, and define the issues in dispute.

For example, it may enable both parties to 'agree quantum subject to liability' before the hearing (see example letter on following page). This means that the parties agree that there is no controversy about the amount of damages claimed on the claim and/or counterclaim, and that the Court need not hear and see evidence (e.g. all the receipts etc) of those damages. Instead, all the Court will have to do is hear evidence of the accident itself and decide on 'liability' i.e. whether a party should pay the claim or counterclaim.

Conversely, the parties may agree at any stage before the hearing that 'liability is agreed' but all that remains in dispute is how much the damages shall be. This is more likely to have been acceded at an earlier stage, when the defendant fills in the Defence form.

Example letter agreeing quantum

WITHOUT PREJUDICE   Miss Joanna Smith
                                                   The Cottage
                                                   Anytown
                                                   AB1 2CD

Dear Mrs Blue

Re: Accident the High Street Anytown at 3 p.m. on 12 January 1999

The quantum of your claim in the Anytown County Court in respect of the above accident (namely £1,322.50) is hereby agreed, subject to liability.

Yours sincerely

Joanna Smith

Joanna Smith

There is no time limit for this sort of agreement and if necessary it can be done at the hearing.

Medical evidence in claim for personal injury

If you are claiming compensation for an injury you have suffered, you must obtain a medical report by a doctor who has examined you to substantiate your injuries. This medical report is filed at the Court together with your Particulars of Claim and County Court Summons (N2). Remember that a copy for the Defendant should also be enclosed.

Relying on criminal conviction of your opponent

If one or more of the parties was convicted of a motoring offence related to the incident which is the subject of a civil claim, evidence of that conviction in the form of a certificate obtained from the convicting Court can be placed before the judge. Such evidence will strengthen the case against the convicted person.

The following is an example paragraph which should be inserted in your 'Particulars of Claim' or 'Defence'.

The [Plaintiff or Defendant] intends to place evidence before the Court pursuant to Section II of the Civil Evidence Act 1968 that the [Defendant or Plaintiff] was on [date] at [name and address of Court] convicted of [name of offence]. The said conviction is relevant to the issue of [the defendants liability for negligent during as alleged above] [the Plaintiff's contributing to and or causing the said accident as alleged above].

You should tell the convicted person that you intend to use the evidence in the Particulars of Claim (if you are the plaintiff) or Defence (plus Counterclaim) if you are the defendant.

Obtaining the certificate

You will need to write to the Court where the party was convicted asking for a certificate of connection for use in civil proceedings. Practice varies from court to court so inquire by telephone to whom the letter should be addressed. The Court will also be able to tell you what fee is payable.

Your letter should include:

    a)   the name of the convicted person;

    b)   the date of conviction (the day the accused pleaded guilty or was found guilty at trial);

    c)   the offence involved.

Challenging evidence of conviction

If you were the convicted person you can challenge the conviction at the civil hearing on one or more of the following grounds;

a)   that you were not convicted as alleged. i.e. the wrong person, court or offence is cited on the certificate, or

b)   that you were wrongly convicted. Note even if you succeed this will not overturn your conviction

c)   the conviction is not and/or relevant to issues in the civil case. i.e. it arose out of a separate incident.

Obtain legal advice. if you want to claim the conviction was wrong. If you state that you were not convicted or that the conviction is not relevant to the civil action you should include the following paragraph at the end of your Defence (and Counterclaim) or your Reply to the Defence/Defence of Counterclaim (see pages 36 and 38).

> The [Defendant or Plaintiff] denies that [he or she] was convicted of [the offence] at [court] on [date] as alleged in the [Particulars of Claim/Defence/Counterclaim] or at all.

or

> The [Defendant or Plaintiff] admits that [he or she] was convicted of [the offence] at [Court] on [date] as alleged in the [Particulars of Claim/Defence/Counterclaim] but denies that the said conviction is relevant to the issue alleged in the said [Particulars of Claim/ Defence/ Counterclaim or to any issue in this action.

The hearing

The hearing will usually take place in front of the 'District Judge', in 'Chambers'. If lawyers attend they will not wear robes. Members of the public and people who are not directly connected with the proceedings are not allowed in. If you have someone you want to attend the hearing you must ask the judge and the other parties if they mind.

Witnesses other than the plaintiff and defendant may be asked to wait outside until called to give evidence.

The hearing will be conducted round a table, although in some County Courts the room may look more like a traditional courtroom. Everyone remains seated. Parties will not usually have to give evidence on oath. The judge is addressed as 'Sir' or 'Madam', as appropriate and has wide powers to conduct the case. His principal duty is to give each side a chance to put his case. The hearing may take the form of a series of questions from the judge; or it may be more formal, with the plaintiff putting his case first and the defendant replying.

It may be helpful to have a checklist of matters you want the judge to hear about, and what evidence you want him or her to consider, as follows:

Plaintiffs list

1. The defendant's driving

    a) My story – how the accident happened caused the accident.
    b) Photographs of the site.
    c) Evidence of Miss Red (independent eyewitness).

2. My car was damaged

    a) Engineers inspection report.
    b) Photographs of car taken by me.
    c) Receipt of payment by me.

3. I suffered whiplash

    a) My story – how injury affected me – injury to my neck.
    b) Medical report from my GP.
    c) Prescription for surgical collar – receipt.
    d) Receipts of painkillers.

Defendant's list

1. The plaintiff's driving caused or partly contributed to the accident.

    a) My version of events.
    b) Miss Red's evidence - how it helps me.
    c) My photographs.

Make sure that you tell the Court everything you have to say. There is nothing more frustrating than walking away and thinking 'if only I had mentioned .....' or 'if the judge had seen the document....'

Use the checklist to avoid this: tick of each item as the judge hears about it. If it seems the other party is doing all the talking be patient! Do not be 'put off' if the other party (plaintiff or defendant) is represented by solicitor or barrister. You are there to tell your story, and the judge is there to hear both sides. Remember not to interrupt, or argue with either the judge or your opponent. It is in your interests to appear calm, confident and reasonable. Getting angry may confuse you, or mean that your evidence is not as clear as it might be. When you get the chance start putting your case methodically, following your check-list. Do not be deflected – deal with questions and interruptions and then move on with your story.

Judgment

After hearing both sides the judge will explain what facts he finds have been proved (e.g. the defendant was driving too fast in the circum-stances ...the plaintiff took a proper course around the roundabout indi-cating left as she did so, etc.). He will then explain which party has won.

Once liability and the amount of damages to be paid has been announced the judge will proceed to calculate:

a) Interest: usually at 8% p.a. from the date of the accident or payment for repair or some other suitable date.

b) Court fee.

c) Witness costs (including travel costs and loss of earnings up to £50). Note: if you took paid holiday to attend the hearing you cannot claim because you have not lost earn-ings.

Any witness on the winning side can claim witness costs.

Normally the 'loser' is not ordered to pay any other costs. However the costs of bringing the case (obtaining legal advice, writing letters, postage, photocopying, film processing) are recoverable where the judge decides there has been 'unreasonable' conduct by one of the parties.

Examples

The examples on following pages are imaginary 'pleadings' arising out of two fictional road traffic accidents.

Accident 1 occurred between a pedestrian and a driver. The plaintiff is the pedestrian suing the driver for damage to property, and a minor personal injury. The defendant is the driver who is resisting the allegations on the grounds that the pedestrian was all or partly to blame for the accident.

Accident 2 is a straightforward minor road traffic accident between two drivers. The plaintiff alleges the defendant's negligence caused the acci-dent and the damage to his car. The sample 'Particulars of Claim' contains various examples of how to plead different accident situations – it would be most unfortunate if all these events happened to cause one accident. The Particulars of Claim also shows how to plead the different type of loss (write-off value of car; cost of repairing the car; policy excess).

This example also shows how a defendant can ask the plaintiff to pay for damage he has suffered – in a document called 'Counterclaim' which is served at the same time as the 'Defence'. The important thing to remember about a 'Counterclaim' is that it is basically a document similar to the 'Particulars of Claim', and is set out in the same way.

Points to remember

1.   Tailor the pleading to suit your circumstances; it is there to tell your story

2.   The 'Particulars of Claim' or 'Defence' should be written on a separate piece of paper and enclose it with the Form 'Request for Summons' (if you are the plaintiff) or Form N9B 'Defence and Counterclaim' (if you are the defendant).

3.   You need not type out the pleading, but if it is hand-written make sure it is legible. Also number all the paragraphs.

4.   Fill in the appropriate forms Form N1 or Form N9B and enclose a copy of your pleading for the court and for each of the parties. Remember that if you have a claim for personal injury you must also enclose copies of a medical report for the court and other parties.

5.   Remember to keep copies of all documents served, with a record of when they were sent.

6.   If you later notice a mistake, inaccuracy or omission you can ask the others side (by letter, or orally at Court) if you can amend your pleading. If the other party does not agree you can ask the District Judge if you can amend at the hearing.

Accident 1: Particulars of claim

Scenario: The plaintiff, Mr Pedestrian, was knocked down by a motorist while crossing a road. His claim is for damaged spectacles and for bruising on his back and side.

IN THE ANYTOWN COUNTY COURT   CASE NO:

BETWEEN   Mr Pedestrian   Plaintiff
                 and
                 Miss Driver   Defendant

PARTICULARS OF CLAIM

1. At about 3.00 pm on 7 January 1999 the Plaintiff was crossing the High Street, Anytown when the Defendant driving a Vauxhall Astra registration number S123 QAZ reversed, causing the said car to collide with the Plaintiff and knocking him to the ground.

2. The said collision was caused by the negligence of the Defendant;
   PARTICULARS OF NEGLIGENCE
   (a) failing to keep any or proper lookout
   (b) failing to have any or sufficient regard for pedestrians crossing the road
   (c) failing to see the Plaintiff in time to avoid colliding with him, or at all
   (d) failing to stop, swerve, steer or control her car so as to avoid colliding with the Plaintiff

3. By reason of the above the Plaintiff whose date of birth is 27 September 1967 suffered injuries loss and damage;
   PARTICULARS OF INJURY
   (a) pain suffering and loss of amenity
   (b) shock
   (c) bruising to lower back and left thigh
   PARTICULARS OF SPECIAL DAMAGE
   (i)   cost of replacing pair of prescription spectacles   £250.00
   (ii) cost of dry cleaning 1 pair of trousers   £12.00
   (iii) cost of pain killers   £3.80
   Total   £265.80

4. Further the Plaintiff is entitled and claims interest on such damages and for such a period as the court may determine pursuant to Section 69 of the County Courts Act 1984

AND THE PLAINTIFF CLAIMS
(1) Damages
(2) Interest pursuant to Section 69 of the County Courts Act 1984

Served the 12 January 1999   by Mr A. Pedestrian   *A. Pedestrian*

Accident 1: Defence

Scenario: Miss Driver in the accident wishes to say that Mr Pedestrian stepped off the kerb without looking, giving him no time to avoid knocking him down. Miss Driver wishes to say alternatively, that in failing to take care of himself he was partly to blame for the accident.

IN THE ANYTOWN COUNTY COURT   CASE NO:

BETWEEN   Mr Pedestrian   Plaintiff

and

Miss Driver   Defendant

DEFENCE

1.   Paragraph 1 of the Particulars of Claim is admitted

2.   It is denied that the Defendant was negligent as alleged in the Particulars of Claim or at all.

3.   The Defendant's case is that the collision was caused by or contributed to by the Plaintiff.

PARTICULARS OF NEGLIGENCE

(1)   Stepping off the kerb into the path of the Defendant's vehicle without giving her reasonable time to avoid the collision

(2)   Failing to keep any or any proper lookout for other road users

(3)   Failing to heed the Defendant's motor car in time or at all

(4)   Failing in all the circumstances to have any or sufficient regard for his own safety when crossing the road or at all.

4.   The defendant does not admit the Plaintiff suffered injury loss and damage and will put the Plaintiff to strict proof of all matters alleged in paragraph 3 of the Particulars of Claim

Served on 1/2/99

by Miss M Driver

Accident 2: Particulars of Claim

Scenario: This is a straightforward claim against a driver in an accident involving two cars. The particulars of negligence list various allegations of negligent driving: not all will be applicable in any one case!

IN THE ANYTOWN COUNTY COURT

BETWEEN   Mrs Joan Smith   Plaintiff
and
Mr Simon Brown   Defendant

PARTICULARS OF CLAIM

1.   At 11.40 am on 11 January 1999 the Plaintiff was driving his Fiat Punto motor car Registration Number R111 ZXC along Cole Avenue, Anytown, when he was involved in a collision with the Defendant who was driving a Renault C5 motor car registration number GHQW 007.

2.   The collision was caused by the Defendant's negligence in that he:

PARTICULARS OF NEGLIGENCE

     (i)   overtook the Plaintiff's vehicle when it was unsafe to do so
     (ii)   crossed into the path of the Plaintiff's correctly proceeding vehicle
     (iii)   failed to maintain lane discipline [on the roundabout]
     (iv)   failed to observe the Plaintiff's right of way when emerging from a side road into Cole Avenue
     (v)   drove too fast at all material times
     (vi)   failed to heed the presence of the Plaintiff's vehicle in time or at all
     (vii)   failed to stop steer or otherwise his control so as to avoid colliding with the Plaintiff's vehicle
     (viii)   failed to comply with the red light signal which was at that time showing to him

3.   By reason of the above the Plaintiff has suffered loss and damage:

PARTICULARS OF SPECIAL DAMAGE

     (1)   [Written off value of the motor car   £1450.00]
     or [Cost of repairs to the motor car   £839.50]
     or [Insurance policy excess   £150.00]

     (2)   cost of taxi cabs used by the Defendant during the three days the motor car was being repaired   £20.40

4.   The Plaintiff claims interest on such damages pursuant to section 69 of the County Courts Act 1984 at such a rate and for such a period as the court thinks fit.

And the Plaintiff claims

     (1)   Damages
     (2)   Interest on damages pursuant to section as of the County courts Act 1984

Joan Smith   Served on 1/2/99 by Mrs Joan Smith

Accident 2: Defence and Counterclaim

IN THE ANYTOWN COUNTY COURT   CASE NO

BETWEEN   Mrs Joan Smith   Plaintiff
                 and
               Mr Simon Brown   Defendant

DEFENCE AND COUNTERCLAIM

1.   paragraph 1 of the Particulars of Claim is admitted

2.   It is denied that the Defendant was negligent as alleged or at all. It is the Defendant's case is that the accident was caused or contributed to by the negligence of the Plaintiff.

3.   [Say how the accident happened, eg:]

      The Plaintiff drove up behind the Defendant who was waiting to proceed onto the roundabout . The Defendant drove on to the roundabout when the way ahead was clear. The Plaintiff then attempted to overtake the Defendant's vehicle by driving alongside him. The Plaintiff then sharply cut in front of the Defendant's vehicle without warning thus causing the two cars to collide.

4.   No admission is made as to the matters pleaded in Paragraph 3 of the Particulars of Claim and the Plaintiff is put to strict proof of each and all of them.

COUNTERCLAIM

5.   The Defendant repeats paragraphs 1-4 above

6.   The Plaintiff was negligent in that she:-

      PARTICULARS OF NEGLIGENCE

      [List the ways in which the Plaintiffs driving fell below standard: see previous pages for examples]

7.   By reason of the matters listed above the Defendant suffered loss and damage:

      PARTICULARS OF DAMAGE

      (1)   cost of repairs to the Defendant's motor vehicle   £2,800.00

      (2)   loss of use of the car whilst it was being repaired – 7 days   £235.17

8.   The Defendant claims interest on such damages pursuant to section 69 of the County Courts Act 1984 at such a rate and for such a period as the Court thinks fit.

And the Plaintiff claims:

(1) Damages and or the sum of £3,035.17

(2) Interest on damages pursuant to section 69 of the County Courts Act 1984

Simon Brown

SERVED ON 1/2/99 by Simon Brown

Chapter

Motoring offences

The aim of this chapter is to:

- Explain how the law deals with motorists who commit offences.

- Outline your options on receiving a Fixed Penalty Ticket, Vehicle defect Notice or Summons.

- Help you decide whether or not you committed the offence you are accused of.

- Help you decide if you need a lawyer.

- Describe a few of the most common offences and defences.

How the law deals with the motorist

These are the ways of being accused of a motoring offence:

At the roadside...

- warning from a policeman and no further action

- Fixed Penalty Ticket or Vehicle Defect Notice

- warning that prosecution is being considered

- arrest and questioning at a police station (available for only the most serious offences)

At home...

- receive 'Notice of Intention to Prosecute' and/or

- receive summons

- arrest on a warrant

The above shows you how the motorist receives his first contact with the criminal justice system. As you can see there are various options open to the police. If you are lucky an officer may simply give you 'a warning' at the roadside and decide to take things no further. The vast majority of the minor offences will be dealt with by way of a Fixed Penalty Ticket or Vehicle Defect Notice. Proceedings in the Courts for more serious offences will be started by a summons asking you to attend at a Magistrates Court on a particular day (see chapter 4).

Fixed Penalty Tickets and how to deal with them

The Fixed Penalty Ticket system was set up to save the expense and delay of taking drivers to court for committing certain offences. The police officer offers the motorist a 'ticket' at the roadside. The motorist can accept it or reject it there and then. If he accepts it, what happens next will depend on whether he is being charged with an 'endorsable' or 'non-endorsable' offence (see below). If he rejects it, or having accepted the ticket at the roadside decides to challenge the accusation by sending off the slip asking for a hearing at the Magistrates Court, he will be sent a summons (see below)

Note: the Fixed Penalty System is discretionary and the police can choose to give a ticket or to prosecute the motorist through the Courts. The system does not apply to many offences, see the table at Appendix 2.

Non-endorsable offences

Offences falling in this category are the less serious offences such as illegal parking and failure to display a tax disc ('excise licence'). Although you will have to pay a penalty within 21 days, currently £20 (£30 for illegal parking in London) no penalty points can be endorsed on your licence. This type of ticket may be affixed to your car if the driver is not present. Having accepted the ticket you can ask instead for the case to be heard in court by sending off the slip within the 21-day time limit.

Endorsable offences

These offences carry not only a penalty (currently £40) but also a mandatory number of penalty points which will be endorsed on your licence. The police officer at the scene will ask to see your licence and if you accept the ticket will ask you to surrender the licence in return for a receipt. The licence will then be sent away to have the penalty points endorsed upon it, after which it will be returned to you. The penalty is payable within 21 days, but if you wish you may instead ask for the case to be heard in court by sending off the slip within the time limit.

If you do not have your driving licence with you when asked to produce it by a police officer you will be asked to produce it at a police station within the next seven days. Note that it is an offence not to comply. The police may then decide whether or not to offer you a ticket when you take your licence to the police station.

Each offence has a specific number of penalty points (see Appendix 2). If a police officer, on examining your licence sees that endorsement for this offence would automatically disqualify you under the 'totting-up system' (i.e. would take the total number of points endorsed on your licence in the last three years to 12 or more: see below) he cannot offer you a Fixed Penalty Ticket. The police will then send you a summons to attend Court.

Failure to pay the penalty

The ticket gives details of how and where to pay the sum. If you do not pay the penalty within the 21-day time limit the police will register the failure as a fine with your local Court. But beware, the sum registered is the penalty plus 50%. So not only is it more expensive to pay late, but the Courts have various way of enforcing payment of fines (see chapter 4: 'Dealing with the Magistrates Court').

Vehicle Defect Notices and how to deal with them

If your vehicle appears to breach regulations relating to maintenance (e.g. defective tyres or faulty lights) the police may give you a Vehicle Defect Notice requiring you to put the defect right. Failure to do so will result in a PG5 Notice being placed on your vehicle. This invalidates your MOT certificate and makes it illegal to drive your car. Ignore these notices and you risk being served with a summons.

Summons

Unless the alleged offences are connected to an accident the police must:

a)   warn the driver at the time of the offence that prosecution for an offence is being or will be considered OR

b)   'serve' (i.e. hand or post) a summons to the motorist within 14 days of the offence being allegedly committed OR

c)   'serve' (i.e. hand or post) a 'Notice of Intention to Prosecute' for the offence within 14 days of the offence being allegedly committed.

It is up to the motorist to prove to the Court that this procedure has not been followed. If the Court thinks it is more likely than not (i.e. satisfied 'on the balance of probabilities') that you are right you cannot be convicted of the alleged offence.

Receiving a summons

A summons will tell you the time, date and the Magistrates Court where the first hearing will be. It will also contain the details of the allegations against you. If you fail to appear at the correct time or appointed day the prosecution are likely to obtain a warrant for your arrest to ensure that you do appear before the Court on the next occasion (see further 'Dealing with the Court').

Arrest

In some circumstances (usually depending on the offence that is alleged to have been committed) a prosecution for a motoring offence may start with the arrest of the motorist. Most commonly, this will happen when a police officer reasonably thinks a motorist who has taken a roadside breath test is 'over the limit'. Where a motorist has refused to take a breath test an officer may arrest him if he reasonably suspects him to have alcohol in his body (slurring speech or breath smelling of alcohol will usually give the drink-driver away).

The police also have power to arrest a motorist at the roadside if they have a reasonable suspicion that he has been involved in one of the most serious driving offences, namely manslaughter, causing death by dangerous driving, causing death by careless driving whilst under the influence of drink or drugs and 'taking a vehicle without the owner's consent' (known as 'joy-riding'). Such offences are outside the scope of this Law Pack Guide. If the police decide to prosecute you they will 'charge' you for the offence and you will be required (remanded) to appear in the Magistrates Court on a particular day in order to answer to the charge. Once your case reaches the Courts the procedure is the same as if the prosecution had sent a summons.

Have you committed an offence?

Before making a decision on whether to challenge a Fixed Penalty Ticket or, if your case is to be dealt with by summons, on how to plead in Court you should bear the following things in mind.

Have the prosecution complied with the correct procedure?

The police must have warned you of their intention to prosecute unless you are being prosecuted for events arising from an accidental collision (see 'Summons' above).

The definition of the offence

The prosecution will have to prove beyond reasonable doubt that you have committed every element of the offence alleged. So for illustration, if you are accused of 'careless driving' the prosecution will have to prove:

■ you were the person driving the car at the time in question

■ that at the time of the offence it was being driven on a road or public place

■ the manner in which you were driving was 'careless' (see below)

If you were driving on private land to which the public have no access, albeit carelessly, the prosecution will not be able to prove a vital element of the offence, and you cannot be convicted.

Often there will be no dispute over some elements of the offence. For example, a motorist might agree that he was riding a motorbike on a road at the time and place alleged, but having looked at the definition of 'careless' (see page 50) disagrees that the manner of his driving was careless. In that situation he must consider the evidence that the prosecution might call to prove that he was careless (police or independent witnesses) and decide whether to plead guilty or not guilty.

Is there a defence?

Even if, on the face of it, you have committed an offence you must consider whether there is a defence to it. If the Court is satisfied that you have a defence you will not be convicted of the alleged offence. You can raise more than one defence to a charge.

Statutory defences

Sometimes a defence is 'built into' the definition of an offence. A good example is 'failing, without reasonable excuse, to provide a specimen of breath when required to do so' (note there is a similar offence in relation to failures to give a specimen of blood or urine). If you can prove to the court that you had a 'reasonable excuse' (they must believe that your claim is probably true) you will have a defence. Remember that what you think is a reasonable and what the Court thinks is reasonable may be two different things. A medical condition or situation of genuine emergency will probably satisfy the Court.

Other defences may be applicable:

Mechanical defect

If you tell the court at trial that a mechanical defect in your vehicle that you had been unaware of, and could not have reasonably been expected to be aware of caused you to drive in that way, it is up to the prosecution to disprove you. This is only a defence to some offences (e.g. dangerous, careless or inconsiderate driving, and failing to observe the pedestrian crossing regulations). If the prosecution do not succeed you will be found not guilty. An example of where this defence might be successful is where the brakes on a car suddenly fail, thus preventing the driver from being able to stop at a pedestrian crossing.

'Duress of circumstances'

This pompous legal phrase really means that the defendant was driven by the extreme situation he was placed in to do something he would not otherwise have done. Basically the law recognises that the driver was impelled to drive the way he did and thus commit a motoring offence by the circumstances of the moment, and will therefore not punish him for it.

Cases where the motorist successfully relied on this defence in the past include a man who drove recklessly in his attempt to escape from a group of people trying to attack him; and a man who drove with excess alcohol only so far as to escape from the people chasing him. Another possible example would be where a motorist has to make a split-second decision to drive in a particular way in order to avoid an accident and in doing so commits an offence. (See the section below 'Do you need a lawyer?')

Automatism

This is nothing to do with robots! Where the motorist is rendered incapable, through no fault of his own, of consciously controlling his vehicle he will not be held liable for an offence he committed at the time. As examples of this are rare the illustrations usually given are somewhat far-fetched, for example being knocked unconscious by a stone or being attacked by a swarm of bees while at the wheel. However this defence will also apply if the offence was caused by the defendant suffering a stroke or epileptic fit. Where such 'automatism' could (or should) have been foreseen and the motorist did not take precautions to avoid it the defence will not stop him from being convicted. (see the section below 'Do you need a lawyer?').

Remember, not knowing the law is no defence!

The Prosecution must prove its case

The prosecution must prove all elements of the case against you 'beyond reasonable doubt', and if they cannot you must be acquitted. It is perfectly proper to 'sit back' at trial and see if the prosecution can make out the case against you, in the same way as it is for you to challenge the prosecution evidence against you.

Consider the evidence against you

Except where the case might go to the Crown Court (see the table at Appendix 2) you will not have an opportunity to know much about the prosecution evidence before the Court takes your plea. Think of the categories of evidence below and think what they might have against you: (be realistic!)

- Your own words noted by the police after you have been cautioned. This includes statements made by you in interview under caution.

- The evidence of police witnesses who attended the scene, or interviewed you.

- Physical evidence (e.g. the print-out of a breath test analysis).

- Evidence of independent witnesses (e.g. a bystander, or another driver who saw what happened).

- Expert evidence from a professional to give evidence on a technical matter (e.g. a doctor who examined the defendant to see if he is or was unfit to drive through drink or drugs, or a motor mechanic who gives evidence as to whether a car did or did not have a mechanical defect – see above).

Credit for a guilty plea

The Courts, when sentencing, will give 'credit for a guilty plea'. This means that if you plead guilty the sentence will probably be reduced. You will get more credit (as much as one-third off the sentence) if you plead guilty at your first or second Court appearance, than if you plead guilty at your trial.

Do you need a lawyer?

A lawyer can help you with two things;

a)   give you advice on whether to plead 'guilty' or 'not guilty'

b)   prepare and conduct your appearances in Court (whether you plead guilty or not guilty).

While most traffic offences can be easily dealt with by the layman, there are some situations where it is sensible to get expert legal advice; particularly where the offence is serious, the penalty severe or where you want to challenge complex prosecution evidence. Much depends on how confident you are in appearing in Court and telling your story. Financial considerations may also influence you.

When to make this decision

1.   **Arrest.** If you have been arrested and taken to the police station the general rule is that you must be offered the opportunity to consult a lawyer – either a solicitor of your own choosing or the 'duty solicitor' in attendance at the police station for free representation. Such situations are outside the scope of this Guide. Of course you need not be represented if you do not wish it.

      Where the case is less serious you will have more time to think, for you will have either received a Fixed Penalty Ticket or a summons which contain the details of what is said you have done. Decide if you intend to deny the allegations by using the checklist below.

2.   **Fixed Penalty.** In the case of a Fixed Penalty Notice the first thing is to decide if you will pay the fine or if you want the case dealt with in Court. If you want to go to Court you must then decide what to plead. Remember, it is not worth going to Court if you intend to admit the offence (i.e. plead guilty) – a punishment imposed by the Court may well be much greater than the penalty offered by the Ticket. Use the checklist below to help you decide if you need a lawyer. Take note of the time limits.

3.   **Summons.** In the case of a summons you will be given a date to appear in Court. You must decide whether you are going to need a lawyer and whether to plead guilty or not guilty. Of course even if you are not represented by a lawyer at first you can always ask the Court at a later stage to give you time (grant an 'adjournment') to instruct one, although you will no doubt be asked to explain why you did not instruct one earlier. Sometimes Magistrates will indicate that in the circumstances you ought to

seek legal representation. The checklist below will help you think about the issues involved in your case and make an informed decision as to whether to seek legal advice or not. Bear in mind that it may take some time to get an appointment to see a solicitor. It is in your interests to get the case disposed of as quickly as possible; asking the Court for more time might hold up things considerably, and may make you open to criticism.

Checklist

Ask yourself the following questions;

1. **Do I plead guilty or not guilty?**

    ■ Identify the offence (see the table at Appendix 2)

    ■ Do I deny the allegation? (see 'Have I committed the offence?')

    ■ Is there a defence? (see 'Have I committed the offence?)

2. **Do I need a lawyer to prepare and conduct my case?**

    This depends on which type of Court will hear your case, how complex the evidence will be and what sentence might be imposed if you are found guilty.

Where will the case be heard?

The majority of motoring offences will be dealt with in the Magistrates Courts. The most serious, however, will be transferred ('committed') to the Crown Court for trial by jury or sentencing in front of a judge. Where an offence is one that can be tried in either court, the defendant has the right to choose to have a jury trial. It will come as no surprise that the Crown Court is more formal than the Magistrates Court and has complex procedural rules, all of which are outside the scope of this Guide. If it seems there is a possibility of your case transferring to the Crown Court, or you want advice on whether to elect jury trial consult a lawyer by visiting a Citizens Advice Bureau, Legal Advice Centre or firm of solicitors. Note that only solicitor-advocates and barristers can represent you in the Crown Court, although if you do not want to instruct a lawyer you can present the case yourself.

Do you need to trace and call witnesses or 'expert witnesses' to give evidence?

A solicitor will be able to help you with the practical difficulties of tracing witnesses and obtaining scientific evidence, taking down witness statements and assessing how helpful the evidence is. Note that this will only be a consideration if you intend to plead not guilty. When there is a guilty plea the Court will not hold a trial, but instead go straight on to sentence you.

Do you need to challenge the evidence of prosecution witnesses?

Challenging the evidence of prosecution witnesses, who may include police officers and scientific experts, is done by 'cross examination' during trial. The cross-examiner, by asking the witness questions, tries to highlight the weaknesses, inconsistencies or unreliability of the witness' evidence. Lawyers have special training in this skill and it is not within the scope of this Guide to replace or reproduce that skill. If challenging the prosecution evidence is at the heart of your case you would be wise to seek legal representation. Again this consideration only applies where you plead not guilty.

What is the likely sentence?

If you pleaded guilty, or if you are found guilty at the trial of your case, the Court will sentence you. It will take into account the gravity of the offence and the personal circumstances of the offender when deciding what type of sentence and the severity of the penalty to impose. To find out the available sentences for various offences see the Appendix. Depending on the offence, you may be facing a term of imprisonment, a substantial fine or disqualification from driving (for a serious offence or for a minor offence under the 'totting up system'). If this is the case, you may want a lawyer to make a 'plea in mitigation' on your behalf, especially if you want to put forward 'special reasons' (see page 74 and 'Sentencing' generally). If you represent yourself you can also make a plea in mitigation (see page 73).

If in doubt ...

If in doubt as to whether you need a lawyer and how to find (and pay for) one ask at a Citizens' Advice Bureau. Like Law Centres and Legal Advice Centres, Citizens' Advice Bureaux are listed in the phone book and are located in many High Streets and all are available to give legal advice and assistance.

Some specific offences

Dangerous driving

Highlight

The Highway Code can be used in Court to illustrate the standard expected of the 'competent and careful' driver

The prosecution must prove that the driver or motorcyclist drove on a road or in a public place 'dangerously', i.e. that his standard of driving fell far below that expected of a competent and careful driver. The Highway Code can be used in Court to illustrate the standard expected of the 'competent and careful' driver. The offence can also be committed if the vehicle was driven when it was in such a bad or dangerous condition that it was obviously dangerous to drive it. 'Road' includes filter roads, pavements and any road to which the public have access.

Factors that may be considered dangerous driving include:

- driving at excessive speed
- driving on the wrong side of the road
- going through a red light
- forcing other drivers or pedestrians to take evasive action
- causing injury to persons or damage to property

If you are accused of this offence the Magistrates may decide that due to the seriousness of the allegations the case should be committed to the Crown Court for trial if you plead not guilty, or for sentence if you plead guilty. If they decide instead that it is suitable to be dealt with in the Magistrates Court you still have the option to choose a jury trial in the Crown Court. It is therefore wise to consult a lawyer if accused of this offence. A lawyer will be able to give you advice on how to plead and make 'submissions' to the Court on where the case should be dealt with and advise you on whether to ask for a jury trial or not.

The maximum sentence a Magistrates Court can pass is 6 months' imprisonment and/or a fine of up to £5000. For more serious cases the Crown Court can punish by up to 2 years' imprisonment (see Chapter 4 for how the Court arrives at its decision and also other sentences such as community service that are available). In addition, the driver will be disqualified (i.e. banned from driving) and must pass an extended driving test, unless there are 'special reasons'; his licence will also be endorsed with 3-11 penalty points.

Careless driving

This offence is committed by someone who drives a motor vehicle on a road or in a public place

a)   without due care and attention or

b)   without reasonable consideration for other road users.

This is self-explanatory, and the difference between careless (or inconsiderate) driving and 'dangerous' driving is one of degree. Again, failure to observe the Highway Code can be used by the prosecution as evidence of carelessness.

Factors that might be considered 'careless' or 'inconsiderate' driving include (although in the circumstances these may also constitute dangerous driving):

■   overtaking on the inside lane

■   tailgating

■   emerging from a side road into the path of a vehicle or pedestrian

■   being distracted by mobile telephone or passengers / tuning radio / reading map

■   causing a minor accident

■   failing to keep a good look out for hazards

This offence will almost always be dealt with by the Magistrates Court. It is currently punishable by a fine of up to £2,500. You may be banned from driving for a period depending on how seriously the Magistrates consider the offence. Your driving licence will be endorsed with penalty points unless you can prove there are 'special reasons' why they should not (see chapter 4 'Dealing with the Magistrates Court'). The points will reflect the seriousness of the offence, with a minimum of 3 and a maximum of 9.

Drink-driving offences

There are four principle offences:

1.   Driving with excess alcohol

2.   Driving etc. whilst unfit to do so through drink or drugs

3.   Failing to provide a 'sample' of breath (roadside breath test)

4.   Failing to provide a 'specimen' of breath, blood or urine.

Driving with excess alcohol

This offence is committed by driving, or attempting to drive, or being in charge of a motor vehicle on a road or public place whilst the alcohol in your breath, blood or urine is 'over the limit'. The limits are:

> 35 microgrammes of alcohol in 100ml of breath
> or 80 milligrammes of alcohol in 100ml of blood
> or 107 milligrammes of alcohol in 100ml of urine.

'Being in charge' means what it says: it includes a person who is in 'control' of the vehicle and is intending to drive it away, even if he or she is sitting in the vehicle or not.

Examples

Mr Green has been drinking all evening. He is just leaving the pub intending to go to his car which is parked outside and drive home when he is arrested The keys are in his hand. This man is 'in charge' of the vehicle!

Mr Blue has been drinking all evening. He is just leaving the pub when he is arrested. He explains that he is waiting for the taxi he just ordered to take him home, and that he gave his car keys to the barman. This man is not 'in charge' of the vehicle!

How do the police test for alcohol concentration?

A police officer who reasonably suspects that a driver

    a)   has alcohol in his or her body
    b)   has committed a traffic offence while the vehicle is in motion
    c)   has been involved in a motoring accident

can require him or her to take a roadside breath test. Failure to do so 'without reasonable excuse' is an offence (see below). If the test is positive, or if you have refused to take one you will be arrested or asked to go to the police station.

At the police station you will be asked to take two breath tests on an approved device. The machine will produce a printout showing your name, the time and the date and the two readings. This will be used as evidence – though the Court will only take account of the lower reading. If for medical reasons the police decide that a breath test is not suitable, or suspect that the machine is not working properly they may require you to give a blood or urine sample. A blood sample must be taken by a doctor, and with your permission. Remember, refusal to give a sample without reasonable excuse is an offence.

If your breath test produces a reading of between 35 to 50 microgrammes in 100 millilitres of breath you must be offered the chance to

Highlight

'Being in charge' means what it says: it includes a person who is in 'control' of the vehicle and is intending to drive it away, even if he or she is sitting in the vehicle or not

replace the specimen with one of blood or urine, which if given will be used instead.

You will be given a printout of the readings or half of the blood or urine sample (so that you can send it away to a laboratory for analysis if you wish challenge the police evidence).

How is drink-driving sentenced?

A conviction for 'driving' or 'attempting to drive' whilst over the limit carries a maximum punishment of 6 months' imprisonment and/or a fine of up to £5,000. You will be banned from driving for at least 1 year and have your licence endorsed with 3-11 penalty points (unless you can prove there are 'special reasons' why the Court should not do so – see chapter 4 'Dealing with the Magistrates Court')

Being in charge whilst over the limit carries a maximum punishment of up to 3 months' imprisonment and /or a fine of up to £2,500. You may be disqualified from driving, and your licence will be endorsed with 10 penalty points (unless there are 'special reasons').

If the driver has a reading of 100 mg of alcohol or more in 100ml of breath there is a significant risk that the Magistrates will impose a sentence of imprisonment.

Driving etc whilst unfit through drink or drugs

This offence is committed by driving, attempting to drive or being in charge of a motor vehicle on a road or a public place whilst 'unfit' through drink or drugs. 'Unfit' means that the motorist's ability to drive properly was impaired. A doctor will usually be called to give evidence of that impairment, having examined the motorist. The Court will also consider the results of any blood breath or urine tests. Remember that medicines (and insulin) count as drugs for the purposes of this offence.

Defences to drink and drugs-related driving offences

The 'hip-flask defence'

If you did not consume the alcohol (or drugs) until after you had stopped (driving, attempting to drive or being in charge of a motor vehicle) you will have a defence. It will be necessary to call an expert witness to give evidence (back calculation of the amount of alcohol or drugs in your body by analysing your metabolic rate) on your behalf. It is wise to consult a lawyer if you wish to run this defence.

Spiked drinks

In practice this is difficult to prove. You will need to prove that you did not know that you were consuming drink (or drugs) and that you had not intended to do so. You should try to obtain evidence (for example an eyewitness) that your drink was spiked or you were given drugs unknowingly. Expert evidence may also be needed to prove by scientific analysis that but for the unknowing intake of alcohol or drugs you would not be over the limit. Again, given the complexities of the evidence in this sort of defence it is wise to consult a lawyer at the earliest opportunity.

No likelihood of driving

This defence is available only for the offence of 'being in charge whilst over the limit'. You must prove to the Court's satisfaction that at the time you were in charge of your motor vehicle and over the limit you did not intend to drive. Simply telling the Court this will not get you very far; you will have to back it up with a detailed explanation of why you were 'in charge' of the vehicle and why you did not intend to drive whilst over the limit. Scientific evidence will have to be called to explain to the Court that you would not have been over the limit by the time you were intending to drive.

Failing to take a breath test

This offence is self-explanatory; the motorist has refused without reasonable excuse to take a roadside breath test when asked to by a constable in uniform. You may also commit it if you simply 'fail' to take the test, which means that for example you have not given a large enough sample for the device to work. See below for what constitutes a 'reasonable excuse'.

The maximum punishment for this offence is a fine currently up to £1000. Your licence will be endorsed with 4 penalty points (unless there are 'special reasons' – see below) and the Magistrates may disqualify the driver (i.e. ban from driving for a certain period)

Failing to give a specimen of breath, blood or urine

This offence is committed when you fail without reasonable excuse to give a specimen of breath, blood or urine for analysis. See below for what the court considers as a 'reasonable excuse'.

Where the driver had been driving or attempting to drive the Magistrates can impose a maximum penalty of 6 months' imprisonment and/or a fine up to £5,000. The motorist will be disqualified for at least one year, and his or her licence will be endorsed with between

3-11 penalty points unless there are 'special reasons' (see chapter 4 'Dealing with the Magistrates Court').

Where the driver had 'been in charge' of the vehicle (see above) the maximum penalties are up to 3 months' imprisonment and/or a fine of up to £2,500. The licence must be endorsed with 10 penalty points unless there are 'special reasons'. The Magistrates can also disqualify the driver.

What is a 'reasonable excuse'?

What you think of as a reasonable excuse, and what the court expects are probably different things! As a general rule only medical reasons (physical or mental) will be accepted (e.g. a chest complaint, or blood disease). You will need to call a doctor as a witness to give evidence that you had a particular complaint at the time, and that the complaint rendered you unable to produce the specimen or take the test, or that taking the test would have been injurious to your health.

Speeding

Driving in excess of the speed limit for that particular road can be dealt with either by a Fixed Penalty Ticket or by summons in Court. Remember also that some types of vehicle may be subject to speed restrictions, no matter what the speed limit of the road (e.g. cars pulling caravans or trailers).

Evidence

You cannot be convicted on the opinion of one policeman (or other witness) alone. Drivers are usually convicted on the evidence of

  a)   the evidence of two witnesses who both saw you speeding on the same occasion

  b)   one witness and the supporting evidence of a stop watch, Vascar gun, radar meter or speedometer

  c)   evidence produced by a speed camera of an approved type.

The speed limit

Most roads will have signs and 'repeater signs' to tell you what the speed limit is, but remember that where the street lamps are placed 200 yards or less apart the limit is 30 mph. The authorities may impose temporary or permanent restrictions on roads, and breach of these will constitute an offence. Remember that each incident of speeding is a separate offence.

UK speed limits

Type of vehicle	Built-up areas	Single carriageways	Dual carriageways	Motorways
Cars	30mph	60mph	70mph	70mph
Cars towing caravans or trailers	30mph	50mph	60mph	60mph
Buses and coaches	30mph	50mph	60mph	70mph
Goods vehicles (under 7.5 tonnes)	30mph	50mph	60mph	70mph
Goods vehicles (over 7.5 tonnes)	30mph	40mph	50mph	60mph

Defences to charges of speeding

If you wish to challenge the charge you must refuse a Fixed Penalty Ticket and ask for your case to go to the Court where you should plead not guilty.

It is, of course, no defence to say 'I didn't see the sign', as the law expects the careful and competent motorist to look out for and obey all traffic signs. However, if there was no traffic sign marking the speed limit (for example if it had fallen down or been taken away) or the speed sign did not comply with the regulations as to colour size and shape the motorist, it seems, has a defence. Of course, you must first find out if the traffic sign did in fact breach the regulations and this will need some research through the Traffic Signs Regulations. Your local library or a university library may be able to help. Remember, you will need to have evidence, e.g. photographs or a letter proving that the sign was not there or did not comply with the regulations. Once you have put your evidence before the Court the prosecution will have to try and prove that the sign was in fact there or did comply with the regulations.

Challenging the evidence of speed cameras, Vascar, radar guns etc

The prosecution must prove that the photograph or readout was produced by an 'appropriate device' and also must produce a certificate signed by a police officer explaining how the photograph or readout was produced. In addition, the prosecution may not use a photograph or readout produced by a device unless they have sent you a copy of it at least seven days before the hearing or trial.

If you wish to challenge the accuracy of such evidence (i.e. you say the camera somehow was wrong) you will probably need to call expert evidence to prove that it was not working or was inaccurate.

Hand-held radar guns are prone to inaccuracy in certain conditions. For

Highlight

The prosecution must prove that the photograph or readout was produced by an 'appropriate device' and also must produce a certificate signed by a police officer explaining how the photograph or readout was produced.

example nearby metal objects in the street, high-voltage power cables, other radar equipment and TV transmitters may all affect accuracy. Obtain a copy of the Home Office publication 'The Speedmeter Handbook', ref 27/92 for guidelines on the use of the approved devices (tel 01727 865051). If there is a risk of an inaccurate reading the Court's attention should be drawn to it at trial.

Requirements to produce documents

If a police officer believes you:

a) are driving a motor vehicle on a road or

b) were driving a motor vehicle which was involved in an accident or

c) committed a motoring offence

he can ask you to produce your driving licence, insurance certificate or MOT certificate. It is an offence not to do so. However it is a defence to produce the required documents at a police station (of your choosing) within 7 days. Usually the police will issue you with an 'HORT 1' form which requires you to do so. If not, you will have to remember yourself. If required to produce your licence you must do so in person; other documents can be sent by post.

If you cannot produce the documents within the 7-day time limit you will not be convicted if you can satisfy a court that you produced them at a police station 'as soon as reasonably practicable' (see below). If you have not been able to produce the required documents at a police station by the date that the police asked the Court to issue a summons, you will have to satisfy the Court that it was not 'reasonably practicable' to do so. Acceptable excuses for not producing the documents in time might be that you left the country or were admitted to hospital for a period before you could go to the police station. You will need to back this up with documentary or witness evidence.

The maximum punishment for these offences is (currently) a fine up to £1000. Magistrates tend to consider this type of offence serious, because the law gives the driver so many chances to produce his or her documents.

Non-valid documents

The principle offences are using a motor vehicle on a road

a) when no insurance policy is in force or

b) when no excise licence (tax disc) or

c) when a test certificate (MOT certificate) is required but not in force.

'Using a motor vehicle on a road' means more than driving it. A vehicle parked on the road (even if it is incapable of being driven), or a car being towed is considered to be 'used'. This offence can be committed by someone who was not even driving; a person who 'causes' or 'permits' another person to 'use' the vehicle on the road without valid documents is also guilty of this offence. Of course, if another person was acting without your permission or knowledge you have a defence as long as you have not 'used' the vehicle yourself.

To avoid conviction you must prove that either you did not 'use' the vehicle, or you did not cause or permit another person to 'use' it or that you did have valid documents. Produce the documents in court. The court will look to see if the document was valid at the time of the alleged offence, and if it was not you will be found guilty. See Appendix 3 for the maximum penalties.

Bicycles, motor cycles and mopeds

Bicycles

There are various offences that apply specifically to pedal cycles. For example it is an offence to ride on the footpath (pavement), as it is to ride dangerously, carelessly, inconsiderately, or under the influence of drink or drugs on a road or in a public place.

The maximum fines available are as follows:

Dangerous:	£2500
Careless:	£1000
Inconsiderate:	£1000
Unfit through drink or drugs:	£1000

The Highway Code contains useful extra information for cyclists, and do not forget that the rules of the road apply to cyclists as well as to other road users.

Motor cycles and mopeds

These are classed as motor vehicles and the offences that apply to car drivers may be committed also by motor cycle and moped users. By law motor cyclists must wear a safety helmet, as must pillion passengers. The penalty for being convicted for failing to wear a helmet is a fine (maximum £500). You may be offered a Fixed Penalty Ticket instead of prosecution through the Courts. Note that followers of the Sikh religion are exempted from the obligation to wear a safety helmet.

Chapter  4

Dealing with the Magistrates Court

All prosecutions for criminal offences begin in the Magistrates Court. You may be required to come back to Court on more than one occasion before the final hearing. The majority of cases remain there with a few more serious cases being passed up ('committed') to the Crown Court to be dealt with.

The purpose of this chapter is to:

- Outline whether you will have to go to Court or whether you can plead guilty by post.

- Describe the layout and personnel of a Magistrates Court.

- Outline what happens when you plead guilty.

- Outline what happens if you plead not guilty.

- Explain how the Courts sentence offenders.

- Describe some of the sentences available, including the penalty points system and disqualification from driving.

Do you have to go to Court ?

Most prosecutions for traffic offences begin by summons. Some of the more serious ones begin with an arrest. By either method you will be given a date on which to appear in a specified Magistrates Court.

If you were arrested for committing an offence you will be either kept in custody (remand) until the next Court session or will be 'remanded on bail'. The police can impose conditions of bail for example (to pay a 'security' to reside at a particular address or to report to a police station). If you are granted bail you must attend Court at the correct time and on the correct day. Failure to do so is an offence called 'failing to surrender', which is punishable by up to 3 months' imprisonment and/or a fine up to £5000.

Pleading guilty by post

This option applies to some offences. If you are accused of an offence in this category the prosecution will send you:

(i)   the summons;

(ii)   details of how to plead guilty by post;

(iii)   a short summary of the circumstances of the offence.

Return the enclosed form indicating you want to plead guilty and state the mitigating circumstances on the form if there is space, or in a separate letter. An example of how to set out a mitigation letter is provided on page 61.

Remember you must enter a guilty plea to each separate summons.

If the offence is endorsable, i.e. with penalty points (see the Table of Offences at Appendix 2 and 3) you must also enclose your driving licence to the Court and tell them your date of birth and sex.

On the day of the hearing the defendant need not be present. In open court the Court clerk will read aloud the charge, and the statements sent in by the defendant. The magistrates will then proceed to sentence. The Court then notifies the defendant of the penalty.

If you change your mind about pleading guilty by post, either by wanting to appear or to plead not guilty, you can write to the court withdrawing your plea. You must then appear in Court on the first hearing date.

The Courts

Magistrates Courts vary widely in their appearance and administration. In many cities the Magistrates Court building will house a number of very busy courtrooms. In smaller towns there may only be one or two courtrooms which may be open only appear on certain days of the week.

The layout of the courtrooms

Although no courtroom looks the same as another each contains the same features, the bench (where the magistrate(s) sits), the dock (where the accused sits), the witness box and benches for the defence and prosecution lawyers, the press and the Prosecution Service representative.

Displayed outside most courtrooms is a diagram showing the layout of that particular Court. If you are in any doubt where to sit the 'list caller' or other Court staff will be able to assist.

Personnel

The magistrates

The magistrates preside over the Court. 'Lay magistrates' are members of the community who volunteer to be unpaid judges in the Magistrates Courts. They receive training but are not qualified lawyers and they sit in a bench of three, headed by the chairman. In some circumstances there may only be two.

Example mitigation letter

[Name]l
[Address]

Dear Sir/Madam,

I wish the Court to consider the following information when dealing with my enclosed plead of guilty by post.

Circumstances of the Offence

[Give details]

My Personal Circumstances

- [Date of birth]
- [Sex]
- [Details of marital status and any dependents]
- [Employment]
- [Details of your income]
- [What you use your car for and whether anyone depends on you having your car]
- [Further information about yourself: e.g. voluntary work, other work in the community]
- [Any other relevant information]

Yours faithfully

[Signature]

A 'stipendiary magistrate' is a qualified and experienced lawyer (barrister or solicitor) who is a full-time professional magistrate. He or she has the same powers as the lay magistrate but presides over the Court alone.

The clerk to the justices

The clerk or deputy has a number of roles, the most important being to advise the magistrates on the law (i.e. the meaning of an offence, relevant case law, available sentence, etc.). Clerks will often deal with the Legal Aid position or 'pre-trial reviews'. It is the clerk who keeps a record of what happens at each hearing, and who reads out the charge and makes enquiries of the listing offence for new hearing dates.

The list caller

A very important person! Usually at Magistrates Courts a number of cases are listed for the same time, e.g. 10 am or 2pm, and the list caller decides on the order in which the cases are heard.

Make sure you arrive in good time and look for your name on the 'daily cause list' ('today's hearings'). This will tell which court your case is heard in. Each courtroom has its own list caller and you must give your name to him and explain if you are representing yourself, are expecting a lawyer, or need to see the duty solicitor. If you need time to apply for Legal Aid, take legal advice or see the prosecutor tell the list caller who (unless the Court is not busy) will point you to the back of the list.

In many Courts reporting to the list caller constitutes answering bail, ('surrendering to custody'). Therefore, if you do not report to the list caller at the right time you risk being prosecuted for 'failing to surrender'.

The prosecutor

The prosecutor will either be a lawyer from the Crown Prosecution Service, (CPS), or an independent advocate employed by the CPS as an agent. The prosecutor is not part of the Court staff, and it is the magistrates job to decide between the prosecution and defence version of events; whether the prosecution has made out its case against the defendant beyond reasonable doubt.

Try to arrive early so that you can have a word with the prosecutor about your case before the Court sits (i.e. before the magistrates come in). He will be able to tell you if the prosecution is ready to go forward, or whether they are asking for 'adjournment' (extra time). If the case is 'triable either way' (i.e. the offence is triable in either the Magistrates or the Crown Court – see Table of Offences at Appendix 2 & 3) ask for copies of the witness statements, interview transcripts and any other evidence (e.g. breathalyser print-outs) being used. This is collectively known as 'advance information' and is designed to help the Court and the defendant which Court the case should be heard if a not guilty plea is entered. If requested, it must be served on the defendant. If this information is not available on request at Court, the prosecutor will ask the Court for an adjournment so this can be sent to you.

Finally it is also worth asking the prosecutor at the earliest opportunity, and before pleas are entered, whether he will accept a guilty plea to a lesser offence (known as a plea bargain). This would be suitable, for instance, where a defendant is accused of dangerous driving and offers a plea to careless driving. This offers a quick disposal to the case, keeps down the costs, and allows the defendant to gain credit for a guilty plea for a less serious offence than that originally charged. If the prosecutor accepts such an offer the original charge will be withdrawn and a new one put before the Court. You must then plead guilty to the new charge.

Demeanour and dress

Although the professionals (lawyers, magistrates and Court staff) will dress formally there is no need for members of the public to do so. However, it is important to treat the Court personnel and the proceedings with respect. Never argue or lose your temper with the magistrates – there is no point in aggravating people unnecessarily. You will have your opportunity to speak and if you have a point to make do so firmly but politely.

When speaking to the bench you should direct your words to the chairman, who is addressed 'Sir' or 'Madam' as appropriate. However, remember all three magistrates will be deciding your case, so do look at the 'wingers' flanking the chairman. Eye contact is very important. Always stand up when addressing the magistrates.

The diagram on the following page summarises the progress of three types of case through the Magistrates Court.

'Summary only' offences take up the bulk of traffic offences, with dangerous driving being the most common 'triable either way offence'. 'Indictable only' offences are only included in the diagram for completeness.

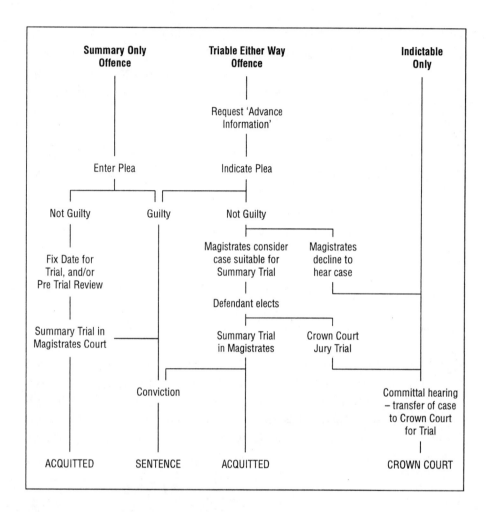

The first appearance

After confirming the defendant's name and address the Court will want to know if the case is ready to be dealt with. It might be that the prosecution need some time to gather more evidence, or that the defendant wishes to apply for Legal Aid, obtain legal advice or consider the prosecution case before entering a plea.

Any party needing extra time can ask the Court to 'adjourn the case' for a specified period (e.g. one or two weeks), and the magistrates can exercise their discretion in granting or refusing such an adjournment. If an adjournment is granted the defendant will be given a date and time on which to return. Usually he or she will be placed on bail – either conditional or unconditional (see below).

If there is to be an adjournment you can take advantage of it and ask the prosecution to furnish you with any evidence (copies of witness statements, printouts from breathalysers, etc.). Whilst the prosecution must comply with your request in a 'triable either way' case (i.e. the offence could be tried either in the Crown Court or the Magistrates Court), it is considered good practice to do so in other cases as well: most prosecutors will be happy to help.

Entering a plea

When all parties are ready the court will formally 'enter' the defendant's plea to each charge. This is done by the clerk reading out the allegation to the defendant who is then asked to plead 'guilty' or 'not guilty', or to 'indicate a plea' for a triable either way offence (see above).

An answer of 'guilty' stands as a conviction and the Court moves to consider sentence (see 'Sentencing').

Entering or indicating a plea of not guilty

In the case of a triable either way offence (e.g. dangerous driving) when you indicate a not guilty plea the Court will then decide where to try the case. The prosecution are asked to give a summary of the facts of the case, and an indication of whether the case is suitable to 'summary trial' in the Magistrates Court. This will depend on the seriousness of the case, and whether the magistrates have sufficient sentencing powers. For the purposes of this decision the prosecution version of events is considered. The defendant (or his lawyer) can address the court on the 'mitigating factors' as appropriate if he wishes to keep the case in the Magistrates Court. Such mitigating factors might include

- dangerous driving alleged was only a brief incident;
- in the circumstances there was little danger to the public;
- the driver had not consumed alcohol;
- no one was injured.

Alternatively, the defendant need make no submissions and if the magistrates 'accept jurisdiction' (i.e. say that the case is suitable for summary trial in the Magistrates Court) he can ask for a jury trial in the Crown Court. When a jury trial is elected or if the magistrates do not accept jurisdiction the Court will set in motion the transfer of the case to the Crown Court, by setting a 'committal date', usually in about 6 weeks' time. Committal hearings and Crown Court trials lie out with the scope of this Guide.

After a plea of not guilty has been entered (or after the Court and defendant have decided the case is suitable for summary trial – see above) the Court will fix a trial date.

Depending on the practice at each Court either a date will be fixed for trial, or additionally a 'pre-trial review' will be ordered. The Court will need to know how many witnesses will be called, and how long the trial is likely to take. You must also be able to tell the Court if you or your witnesses have any 'dates to avoid'. Remember to tell the Court of any hospital appointments, holidays already booked, etc.

A pre-trial review appointment is designed to smooth out any difficulties before trial. Various things may be sorted out including:

- confirming the number of witnesses;

- whether interview transcripts can be read or whether tapes need to be played at trial;

- if anything is agreed between the prosecution and defence e.g. the ownership of the vehicle registration number of the vehicle, and the place and time of the incident;

- confirming the trial date.

Remember, you may wish to plead guilty to some of the charges and not guilty to others. If this happens the Court could sentence you immediately for the offences you have admitted, or the magistrates might put them over for sentencing immediately after the trial for the not-admitted offences. It may even be appropriate to order pre-sentence reports in the meantime. If you are acquitted at trial the Court will deal with the matters you pleaded guilty to in the normal way (see 'how magistrates decide upon sentence').

The trial

No book can give the definitive guide on how to conduct a trial. The following paragraphs aim to give you some idea of what to expect at the hearing, outline the structure of the trial and provide a list of dos and don'ts. If you are not represented by a lawyer at trial the clerk to the justices can help by asking the prosecution witnesses questions: no-one expects you to produce brilliant cross-examination without any practice.

The hearing will be held in the courtroom. Witnesses wait outside until they are called to give evidence, which they do 'on oath' or after 'affirming'. As before, either two or three 'lay' magistrates or one 'stipendiary' magistrate will hear the case. The party addressing the Court stands up to do so, though witnesses may be invited to sit in the witness box to give evidence.

The structure of the trial

The trial will invariably be in the following order:

(1) Opening speech by the prosecution (summarising the facts and explaining any law).

(2) Prosecution evidence in the form of:

   (a) 'live' witnesses (oral evidence);

   (b) 'section 9' witness statements (read aloud by the prosecutor);

   (c) interview transcripts (if agreed by the defence);

   (d) tape or video evidence;

   (e) 'real evidence' (e.g. relevant documents, breathalyser printouts, other exhibits).

(3) Defence evidence, usually consisting of live evidence of the defendant and any other of the categories of evidence listed at (2) above

(4) Defence closing speech, in which the defence outlines to the magistrates:

   (a) the facts on which the prosecution evidence is 'weak' (e.g. witnesses giving incredible or inconsistent testimony);

   (b) matters which make the defendant's case stronger and his evidence (and that of his witnesses) more credible; including a lack of previous convictions:

   (c) a reminder that the prosecution must prove the case 'beyond reasonable doubt', and that the defendant need only prove a defence (see list of defences in chapter 2) on the 'balance of probabilities'; remember this is an opportunity to summarise and persuade, not to give evidence all over again!

Giving evidence

The oath or affirmation

A witness will be asked by the usher what religion he is or whether he would prefer to 'affirm'. If he wishes to take the oath he will be handed the appropriate Holy Book and asked to read the words on a card provided aloud. The affirmation is made in the same way, without the

Holy Book and with slightly different wording. Whether the witness affirms or takes an oath the evidence given will be 'sworn testimony' and the solemnity of the promise to tell the truth is the same.

Testimony

The witness is there to tell the Court of his knowledge and perception of the events that are to be considered. There may be many things he cannot tell the Court about, because he simply does not know about them or did not notice. Remember, you cannot tell the Court what somebody else has said to you about the matters before the Court – this is known as the 'hearsay rule'.

For example, you are accused of careless driving: you cannot tell the Court that a woman pedestrian who witnessed the accident said to you after the accident 'I saw it all happen: the other driver was driving too fast; he was to blame, not you'.

Only she can give evidence of what she saw – you cannot. This means that tracing eyewitnesses who can help you is very important. In that situation her evidence that the other driver's excessive speed caused the accident would support your evidence that, despite your maintaining a good lookout, the other driver 'came out of nowhere' to cause the accident.

Tell the Court the story. Remember to include relevant background details such as road conditions, the purpose of your journey, registration numbers of vehicles. It may help to illustrate your evidence with maps, a plan or photographs. Ask the prosecutor if he or she minds first.

Finally, don't forget to show the magistrates any relevant documents or other items of evidence. The Court will mark these as your exhibits.

Your evidence should tell your version of events and if possible answer any questions thrown up by the prosecution evidence. After you have given evidence the prosecution will cross-examine you. This involves being asked a series of questions. The important thing is to be clear about your story; if what the prosecutor suggests is wrong or misleading say so. Try not to get flustered even if you sense the prosecutor is deliberately trying to make you lose your cool. Remember also that important though it is to stick to your guns, do not be unreasonable. If it is pointed out that you cannot be sure of a certain fact agree if this is the case. You will get nowhere if you continue to assert a perfect memory and acute observational powers; the danger is that your story may look manufactured.

Highlight

Remember, you cannot tell the Court what somebody else has said to you about the matters before the Court – this is known as the 'hearsay rule'

Dos and Don'ts

1) Do prepare your evidence in advance.

   ■ Make a list of the relevant facts you want to tell the Court about.

   ■ Have originals of all the documents you want the Court to see, take them with you to the witness box!

   ■ Think about who the prosecution witnesses are and what they will say.

2) Do take notes in Court.

   ■ If you take a note of the prosecution evidence you will be able to refer the magistrates to any incredible or weak testimony.

   ■ It is also helpful to jot down ideas for your closing remarks as they occur to you during the hearing.

3) Do keep calm – don't lose your temper.

4) Do keep in mind the elements of the offence, don't get distracted by irrelevant side issues or a sense of grievance.

Sentencing

There are three elements to the structure of a punishment for a road traffic offence:

1. A penalty for the offence (fine, imprisonment etc.)

2. A penalty in relation to the driving licence (disqualification, penalty points)

3. Other orders such as compensation for property damage or personal injury, or a contribution to prosecution costs.

These are discussed in turn below. Together they make up the sentence, but a sentence will not necessarily be composed of these types of orders. The Tables in Appendices 2, 3 & 4 describe the maximum penalty available for some of the most common offences.

Types of penalty

Absolute discharge

This is where the Court orders no penalty for the offence (although it may be combined with 'driving licence' penalties or compensation orders) and cost orders.

Conditional discharge

The Court imposes no penalty for the offence (although it might impose a 'driving licence penalty' or 'other order' – see below) . However, the Court will also specify a period and if the offender commits any new offence within that period he will be re-sentenced for the original offence by the Court dealing with the new offence.

Fines

This is self-explanatory. The amount of the fine will reflect the seriousness of the offence and the means of the offender. The Court may accept an offer by the offender to pay in instalments and usually a weekly amount will be fixed. Payment is made to the fines office of the Magistrates Court imposing the sentence. However you could ask the magistrates to transfer payment to a more convenient Magistrates Court.

Community penalty

This category includes 'probation order' and community service orders. A probation order requires the offender to submit to the supervision of a probation officer for a period time (between 6 months and 3 years). There may be a condition to attend a drug or alcohol dependency programme. Proposals for such supervision will be contained in the 'pre-sentence report' prepared by the probation service.

Community service orders require the offender to spend a specified number of hours doing unpaid work in the community. The probation service supervises such an order, and will have considered the suitability of the offender and the availability of projects in a pre-sentence report.

It is also possible to combine both probation and community service order (called a 'combination order').

Imprisonment

This penalty is self-explanatory. The maximum length of imprisonment for selected offences is shown in the Tables at Appendix 2 & 3.

This will be imposed where the Court thinks the offence(s) is so serious that only custody can be justified. It is very rare for the maximum term to be imposed.

Licence-related penalties

Disqualification from driving

Some offences provide for the immediate disqualification from driving. The Court may have a discretion to disqualify but for some offences they must disqualify ('obligatory immediate disqualification').

Highlight

Community service orders require the offender to spend a specified number of hours doing unpaid work in the community

The other circumstance in which the Court must disqualify a driver is when a licence is endorsed with 12 or more penalty points during a three-year period (the 'totting-up procedure'). See also the new regime for totting up points by newly-qualified drivers below.

Obligatory immediate disqualification

The magistrates or Crown Court must disqualify the driver for at least a minimum period unless there are 'special reasons' not to do so (see below). The minimum periods are:

(i) at least 12 months or

(ii) at least two years where the driver is convicted of manslaughter, 'causing death by dangerous driving', or 'causing death by careless driving whilst under the influence of drink or drugs', having previously been disqualified for 56 days or more in the last three years; or

(iii) at least three years where the driver is convicted of 'causing death by careless driving whilst unfit through drink or drugs', or drink driving, or failing to provide a specimen plus an obligatory disqualification offence, having previously been convicted of any of these offences within the last 10 years.

Offenders convicted of drink-driving offences may be offered a reduced period of disqualification for attendance on a course designed to address the problems and behaviour of drink-drivers. It is up to the offender to pay for such a course; the Court should inform him what they are at the time of sentencing. The offender must consent to the proposal before the Court can order it. Unfortunately courses are not available all over the country. Usually the pre-sentence report (see below) will inform the Court as to the availability of such a course in the locality.

Discretionary immediate disqualification

This is where the Court, taking into account the circumstances of the offence and offender decides that disqualification is appropriate punishment. There are no maximum and minimum periods of disqualification.

Penalty points and disqualification under the 'totting-up' procedure

Will points be endorsed on the driving licence? If the offence causes penalty points (see the Tables of Offences at Appendices 2-4) the driving licence will be endorsed by the Court unless:

(i) the Court disqualifies the driver for that particular offence (obligatory or discretionary immediate disqualification, as above); or

(ii)   more than one 'endorsable' offence has been committed on the occasion in question, in which case only the penalty points relating to the offence which was given the highest number of points are endorsed;

(iii)   there are 'special reasons' (see below).

How many points are endorsed?

Each point-carrying offence incurs either a fixed number of points or a number decided by the magistrates within a range to reflect the seriousness of the offence.

How does 'totting-up' work?

The Court then adds up the points endorsed on the licence within the last 3 years (or since the last totted-up disqualification if less than 3 years ago). If the number of points totted up is 12 or more (see below for the rules relating to newly-qualified drivers) the offender will be disqualified for:

(i)   at least 6 months, or

(ii)   at least 1 year if the driver has previously received a disqualification of 56 days or more in the last 3 years, or

(iii)   at least 2 years if the driver has previously received two or more disqualifications each of 56 days or more in the last 3 years.

The only way to avoid such a disqualification is for the offender to approve to the court these are 'mitigating grounds' (see below).

Newly-qualified drivers

In the first two years after passing a driving test a driver is 'newly-qualified'. If the number of points accumulated during this period is 6 or more the offender's driving licence will be revoked and he or she must undergo a retest in order to obtain a new full driving licence.

How magistrates decide on what sentence to impose

The magistrates must take into account the seriousness of the offence and the circumstances of the offender. Sentencing an offender will take the following course:

(1)   Hear the facts of the offence(s) from the prosecutor (unless there has just been a trial on these matters).

(2)   Hear a list of previous convictions, again read out by the prose-

cutor – the prosecutor should show these to the offender to agree or disagree.

(3)   The reading of any pre-sentence report ordered by the Court on a previous occasion and prepared by the Probation Service after interviews with the defendant.

(4)   Remarks made by the offender (or his lawyer) – also known as a 'plea in mitigation'.

Making a plea in mitigation

(1)   Tell the Court about the background to the offence itself (unless it was all heard by the same magistrates at the trial).

(2)   Inform the Court of your personal circumstances. Cover the following matters:-

- domestic circumstances (spouse or live-in partner, dependant children);

- employment;

- finances (it is sensible to give the Court details of your monthly outgoings and an idea of your monthly disposable income);

- any consequences to you as a result of the offence (such as an injury sustained by you, the affect on family life or job, any letter of apology sent by you to the victim or other people involved, etc.);

- any 'special reason' why the magistrates should not disqualify you or endorse your licence – see below;

    or, any consequence to you of losing your licence under the totting-up scheme or discretionary disqualification (e.g. may lose your job, the harm suffered by someone who relied on you to have your licence);

- tell the Court of anything you have done to address your behaviour or driving skills, e.g. attending treatment for alcohol problems, undertaking voluntary driving lessons, etc;

- apologise to the Court.

Remember, this is not the time to assert your innocence, or to put forward a defence. It may be useful to make a list of what you want to say in order that you do not miss anything out. The more information the Court have about you and the offence the more likely the penalty will be suitable. If you do not give the magistrates this sort of information they will not hear it at all.

Special reasons

There is a very narrow definition of 'special reasons'. It means a circumstance or feature of the offence, not a circumstance relating to the offender. The following may qualify as special reasons:

■   Drinks laced with alcohol without the defendant's knowledge.

■   Driving whilst over the limit due to an emergency.

It is likely that you will be required to produce evidence to back up your story and the Court will make an appointment for a hearing on this issue.

Chapter 5

Parking

Where can I Park?

On-street parking

Metered This is provided by Local Authorities who designate areas and impose restrictions (e.g. limiting the time allowed, limiting use to certain categories of person or vehicle). Parking meters require you to pay an 'initial charge', and an 'excess charge' if you stay longer than you paid for.

Usually road markings show the parking spaces but do remember to read the sign posts, which will tell you of the restrictions in force. If an area is 'designated' by the Authorities the restrictions are not lifted by the suspension of a parking meter. Therefore, if you park at a meter that is covered by a bag or other notice you may still be committing an offence if you park there, depending on the wording of the relevant designation order. Copies of the designation Order are available from the police or Local Authority.

The law is strictly enforced and it is no defence that you had to 'run and get change for the meter' etc. Often meters or ticket machines only operate during certain hours, so read the signs telling you about the restrictions and charges.

Permit system These schemes are also run by Local Authorities which may limit parking to certain categories of vehicles or persons (e.g. 'residents only'). Note the permit system may not operate all the time (e.g. non-permit holders may be able to park in these places at certain times). As before, watch out for signs that tell you about the restrictions.

Off-street Parking

This is provided by Local Authorities or private firms licensed by the Local Authority. Most of these will have ticket machines or payment kiosks.

Yellow lines

Double

These mean that you cannot wait or park on that particular stretch of road at any time.

Single

These mean that you can only wait or park at permitted times. Look out for signposts that tell you what the prohibited times are.

Remember that there may be 'no waiting' or 'no stopping' signs signs marking the entry onto a stretch of road to which restrictions apply. Watch out for them, as yellow lines are only a guide. However, if the signs are not there or do not comply with the regulations you may have a defence.

Red Routes

These are designated 'priority routes' in London designed to keep traffic flowing. They are patrolled by the police.

Who is responsible for the parked vehicle?

The person who last drove the car (i.e. the person who parked the vehicle) is legally responsible for complying with any regulations in force.

Example

Mr A drives into town and finds a parking space at a meter. He has arranged that his wife will pick the car up and drive it home, using the spare set of keys. He places coins in the meter, but Mrs A is delayed by a telephone call and arrives late to collect the car. Mr A is the person who is legally responsible for the excess charge incurred.

What do I do if I get a parking ticket?

Excess Charge Notice

Read the Notice carefully. It will give you details of how much is owing and how you can pay it. Failure to pay the excess charge in time is an offence punishable by a fine (maximum £500). If you have committed this offence whilst using a 'disabled-only' space without being an orange badge-holder yourself then the maximum fine is £1000 (see below). As well as the fine, the unpaid excess charge will also be payable. The sensible course is therefore to pay the charge and avoid going to Court, unless you think you have a defence and will be found not guilty.

Fixed Penalty Notice

This will be offered as an alternative to receiving a Court Summons when a police officer or traffic warden considers you have committed an offence; for example unpermitted parking on yellow lines; breaching regulations for on- or off-street parking places. The Notice will be handed to you, or can be affixed to the windscreen of your vehicle. The penalty payable for parking offences is:

Illegal parking on a Red Route	£40
Illegal parking in London	£30
Illegal parking elsewhere	£20

On receiving a Fixed Penalty Notice you have the following choices:

1.   Pay the charge immediately to the clerk of the relevant Court;

2.   Request that the magistrates hear the matter, and plead 'not guilty' (see chapter x for details). Although you can go to Court in order to enter a 'guilty' plea, this is generally not advisable because unless you have very strong 'mitigation' to tell the Magistrates about, you are likely to get a fine higher than the £20 or £30 Fixed Penalty <u>as well as</u> payment of a contribution towards Prosecution costs.

3.   Do nothing, and wait for the police to send you a further Notice (requesting payment of the penalty or information as to who is the owner of the vehicle) – if this Notice is ignored the Police will register the penalty as a fine at the Court. The amount of such a fine is 50% above the Fixed Penalty. The Court will then start 'fine enforcement proceedings' and will fix a hearing for you to appear before the Magistrates.

Quite simply, to avoid the expense and trouble of going to Court pay any parking tickets or comply with any notices within time!

What do I do if I receive a summons?

Parking offences are treated in the same way as other criminal offences. See chapter 4 for details of how to deal with a Summons. Most common parking offences are punishable only by fine. The following table show the maxima for selected offences:

parking or waiting on yellow lines	£1000	Fixed Penalty Notice available
breach of on-street parking regulations	£500	FPN available
abuse of disabled parking space and breach of on-street parking regulations	£1000	FPN available
breach of off-street parking regulations	£500	
abuse of disabled parking space and breach of off-street parking regulations	£1000	
failure to pay initial charge at parking meter	£500 plus initial charge	
failure to pay excess charge at parking meter	£500 plus excess charge	

What do I do if my vehicle is clamped?

The police and authorised persons may clamp ('immobilise') vehicles that are illegally parked (ie in breach of a statutory regulation). They also have the power to move your vehicle to another part of the road, or another road altogether, and then clamp it. However, if your vehicle is at an on-street parking meter where the initial charge was paid up you cannot be clamped unless 2 hours (15 minutes in London) have elapsed from the end of the period paid for. Disabled orange-badge holders are exempt from being clamped.

A notice will be fixed to the vehicle telling you how to get it released. Not surprisingly, a charge is payable. Currently that charge is £38. Note that it is an offence to interfere with the clamping device, or the notice.

The current law on 'private' wheel clamping is not clear. Some cases recently have described how vehicle owners parked on 'private land' (i.e. not a highway or authorised car park) and have been charged very high release and storage fees. Without clear guidance on whether this is lawful from the Courts the wisest measure is to avoid such parking places. Do not park where you are not authorised to do so. If there are clear warning signs to motorists on the private land that unauthorised cars will be clamped you are deemed to have consented to run the risk of being clamped if you are parked there without authorisation. Note in Scotland such private clamping is considered extortion and theft and is therefore not lawful.

What do I do if my vehicle is towed away?

The Authorities may remove vehicles that are parked illegally, obstructively or dangerously on a road, or seem to have been abandoned. The vehicle may be moved to another part of the road or removed to a place of custody. In order to recover your vehicle you must satisfy the authorities that you are the owner of the vehicle and pay the various sums charged;

a)   storage (at a daily rate)
b)   removal fee
c)   a penalty may also be payable in Greater London.

This can work out very expensive. If there has been a mistake for some reason you will have the chance to make representations to the authorities and ultimately to the Parking Adjudicator. If you are successful you may get any sums you have paid out refunded.

Exemptions for disabled drivers

If you hold an 'orange badge' issued by the Local Authority you will be exempt from certain restrictions applying to on-street parking (and may be exempt from some restrictions applying to off-street parking). There is no charge or time limit for on-street metered parking places. Where there is a 'limited waiting order' there is no time limit, however in a 'No Wait' zone the limit is three hours and you must display the time disc correctly.

Chapter

Motoring abroad

Your insurance company or car-hire company will be able to give you comprehensive advice about motoring abroad, however the following is a general guide to what you must consider before you go.

Driving licences

1. New-style Full British Licence (pink and green); this is acceptable in all EU countries. In other countries an International Driving Permit may be necessary (see below).

2. Old-style Full British Licence (green); this is accepted alone in most EU countries and Scandanavia. In Austria a further form of ID with a photograph is required, and in Italy, Portugal, Spain, an International Driving Permit is required. In other countries around the world an International Driving Permit may be necessary.

3. International Driving Permit; this is obtainable from the large motoring organisations (RAC and AA) for a small fee and is acceptable world wide. Indeed, where a British driving licence is not acceptable (see above) an IDP is a necessity. It is also a useful form of general ID as it contains your photograph. It it valid for one year.

Insurance

As in the UK, motor insurance (third party, fire and theft) is compulsory in the EU and other countries. It is very important to check with your insurer that you are covered for the country you will be driving in. It may be sensible to have a more comprehensive cover than the minimum legally required (to cover your own expenses, such as the cost of repairs, legal expenses and alternative transport arrangements etc).

Proof of your Insurance cover should be carried with you. A Green Card (International Motor Insurance Certificate) is not compulsory in EU countries, but it is internationally recognised, and may be more readily understood where there is a language barrier. A Green Card can be obtained from your insurer on request.

Proof of ownership

When travelling abroad make sure you take your V5 document. This is sent to you by the DVLA on registration. It proves that you are the registered owner and keeper of the vehicle. If yours is mislaid you can obtain a 'Certificate of Registration'; from the nearest Registration

Office for a small fee. If your vehicle is hired you need to obtain a 'vehicle of hire' certificate (VE 130) from the AA or RAC proving that you have permission to take the vehicle from the UK. Check with your hire company for further details.

Other requirements

Before you drive abroad, especially if you are unfamiliar with driving conditions there, check if there are other compulsory requirements or restrictions. Your insurance company may be able to give you this information, otherwise the relevant emabassy or tourist offices should be able to help.

Common compulsory requirements are;

- GB sticker
- First Aid kit
- Fire extinguisher
- spare set of light bulbs
- warning triangle.

Remember that speed limits will be different and usually expressed in kilometres per hour, and that maximum alcohol limits will vary from country to country. Laws governing the minimum age of the driver and the wearing of seat belts may also differ.

The following table shows some of the characteristics of motoring laws in popular destinations in Europe.

What to do if you have an accident abroad

This Guide cannot give advice on the law in countries abroad. However, the advice to motorists remains the same as it would be for this country;

- exchange details with other parties involved
- obtain names and addresses of any witnesses
- take photographs or a video recording of the scene
- write down your recollection of what happened
- take down the details of any police officers or other authorities involved
- contact your insurer.

Another useful source of advice is the local British Embassy (or High Commission, depending on which country you are in). Additionally, major cities may have a British Consulate where practical help and advice may be sought (eg legal representation and translation services). These services will cost money, so the best course is to have obtained wide insurance cover prior to leaving on holiday.

Caravans and camper-vans

A caravan is deemed to be a 'trailer' for the purposes of road traffic law in the UK. Lower speed limits apply when one is being towed;

Built up areas:	30mph
Single carriageways:	50mph
Dual carriageways:	60mph
Motorways:	60mph

Contact the RAC or AA for details on speed limits abroad.

A 'camper-van' or motor-caravan (up to 3.05 tonnes unladen) is subject to no separate speed restrictions.

It is an offence to allow a vehicle or trailer (i.e. caravan) to be on a road which poses a threat of injury to any person by virtue of its condition, load, carriage of passengers or the purpose for which it is being used.

European motoring regulations

Country	Minimum driving age	Licence Documents	Maximum speed limit Kph (Mph)			Blood-alcohol units	Compulsory equipment	Other
			Built up	Trunk Rd	Motorway			
Austria	18	New style pink & green licence *or* old style green UK licence	50 (31)	100 (62)	130 (81)	0.08%	Warning Triangle, First Aid Kit, GB Sticker	seat belts must be worn, under 12s must use appropriate child seats in the front, a motorway tax sticker must be displayed on certain motorways
Belgium	18	Full UK licence	60 (37)	90 (56)	70-120 (43-57)	0.8%	Warning Triangle, GB Sticker	seat belts must be worn, no under 12s in the front seat unless there is no adequate room in the back
France	18	Full UK licence	50	90/110	130	0.08%	Warning Triangle, if your vehicle has no hazard lights, GB sticker	seat belts must be worn, under 10s must use child seats
Germany	17	Full UK licence	50 (31)	80 (50)	130 (81)	0.08%	Warning Triangle, GB sticker	seat belts must be worn, under 12s must use appropriate child seats in the front
Greece	18	Full UK licence	50 (31)	80 (50)	100 (62)	0.05%	Warning Triangle, Fire Extinguishers, First Aid Kit, GB Stickers	no under 10s in the front seat,
Italy	18	New style pink & green licence *or* old style green licence and IDP	50 (31)	90 (56)	110/130 (68)/(81) (The lower speed limits applies to vehicles under 1100cc)	0.08%	Warning Triangle, GB sticker,	under 12s sitting in the front should be adequately restrained, seat belts must be worn
Ireland (Eire)	17	Full UK licence	(30)	(60)	(70)	0.08%	GB sticker	
Netherlands	18	Full UK licence	50 (31)	80 (50)	70*-120 (44)*-(74) *NB: compulsory minimum speed	0.05%	Warning Triangle, GB Sicker	No under 12s in the front seat, Seat belts must be worn
Spain	18	New style pink & green licence *or* old style green licence and IDP	50 (31)	90 (56)	120 (74)	0.08%	set of replacement bulbs, GB sticker	under 12s sitting in the front should be adequately restrained, seat belts must be worn
Scandinavia	18 17 in Norway	Full UK licence	50 40 in Finland	60 70 in Sweden	110 90 in Norway	0.05% 0.02% in Sweden	Warning Triangle, (Denmark & Sweden)	headlights must be switched on when you drive at all times (Sweden & Norway), seat belts must be worn
Switzerland	18	Full UK licence	50 (31)	80 (50)	120 (74)	0.08%	Warning Triangle, First Aid Kit, GB Sticker	seat belts must be worn in the front, Motorway tax sticker must be displayed if travelling on motorway, under 7s sitting in the front seat must be adequately restrained
Portugal	17	New style pink & green licence *or* old style green licence and IDP	50 (31)	90-100 (56-62)	120 (74)	0.05%	Warning Triangle, GB stickers	

Chapter  7

Nuisance and the motorist

Road rage

'Road rage' is a term that has come into general use in recent years to describe aggressive driving or other behaviour in motorists directed towards other road users.

Common examples of types of road rage include;

- tailgating (driving very close to the car in front)
- flashing headlights
- hooting
- making offensive gestures
- verbal abuse
- physical assault
- chasing

Such behaviour tends to be directed to another driver or road user in order to intimidate or 'punish' him or her. However deserved such behaviour may seem to be, it is inexcusable and in criminal proceedings will be seen to be an aggravating feature. It follows that road rage incidents will be considered as more serious by the Courts than straightforward incidents of 'bad' or inattentive driving. More importantly, road rage can be extremely dangerous (e.g. tailgating or chasing).

What to do if you suffer a road rage incident

Of course, road rage covers a wide range of behaviour, from the minor and merely aggravating to the very dangerous. Obviously, in a very serious incident where an assault or accident occurs the emergency services will attend. In less serious cases it is open to you to report the matter to the police in the normal way. Remember that there is no offence of road rage as such, but that the other driver's behaviour may amount to one or more of the following criminal offences;

- dangerous driving
- careless driving
- inconsiderate driving
- assault, etc.

The most important thing to do is to keep calm and avoid reacting angrily and aggressively yourself. To do so inflates the situation and puts you and other road users in danger. Try not to take offensive behaviour personally. Most 'road rage' incidents resolve as drivers move away from each other. Try not to be rattled by what has just happened; keep your attention on your own safe driving. If necessary take

---

Highlight

Most 'road rage' incidents resolve as drivers move away from each other. Try not to be rattled by what has just happened; keep your attention on your own safe driving

a break for a few minutes to recover your composure. Never take out your feelings on other drivers – by doing so you will be perpetuating road rage behaviour yourself.

An unfortunate minority of road users falls victim to more serious road rage incidents. If this happens to you try to keep calm and concentrate on driving to a safe place. Your priorities should be

    a)   to avoid being or seeming confrontational

    b)   to maximise your safety

The Automobile Association recommends the following steps:

- avoid making eye contact with your agressor;

- do not attempt to accelerate or swerve suddenly;

- if you are being followed or the driver continues to hassle you, drive to the nearest police station or busy place to get help;

- lock your car doors and keep windows and sunroof only partly open;

- when stopped in traffic, leave enough space to pull out from behind the car in front of you;

- if anyone tries to get into your car, attract attention by sounding your horn or a personal alarm;

- do not be tempted to 'have a go' and do not carry any sort of weapon, which may provoke further anger and end up in the aggressor's hands.

A Road Rage report produced by the AA is reproduced in Appendix 5.

Road rage and mitigation in the criminal Courts

If you plead guilty to an incident characterised by road rage, or are found guilty after a trial you will have the chance to speak about the offence and your personal circumstances (mitigation).

Explain to the court what aroused your anger, and tell them of any steps you have taken to address this. Such steps might be:

- taken advice or counselling on anger-management;

- taken steps to address underlying problems e.g. stress or tiredness while driving;

- undertaken driving lessons to 'rectify' bad driving habits.

If you pleaded guilty:

- written an apology letter to the 'victim' (via the prosecution, police or Court)

If you pleaded not guilty and were found guilty :

- apologise orally to the victim if he/she is in Court, or if not express your intention to do so

Remember to provide evidence to back up your statements, e.g. letter from your doctor or driving instructor and copies of any apology letter sent to the victim.

For serious incidents of 'road rage' where an assault is alleged it is wise to obtain legal advice and representation. This is because the Court has indicated that custodial sentences are appropriate for such cases.

For further information about the criminal Courts see chapters 3 and 4.

Noise nuisance and the motorist

Car alarms, loud noise and music coming from vehicles may amount to a nuisance – i.e. interfering with the personal comfort of people living nearby. Your Local Authority has a duty to take reasonable steps to investigate a complaint, and if they believe the noise is a nuisance they will serve an 'abatement notice' on the person responsible.

An abatement notice can be affixed to the offending vehicle or given to the driver, (or the person who is the registered owner at the DVLA). It will require the 'responsible person' to stop the thing that is causing the nuisance or to take other specified steps within a certain time. To appeal an abatement notice served on you you can do so to a Magistrates Court within 21 days. You might want to do this where you are not the 'responsible person', for example. If you ignore the Notice and do not comply with its requirements you are committing an offence. This can mean heavy penalties – a maximum fine of £5000 and a daily fine for each day the nuisance continues after conviction.

If the abatement notice has not been complied with the Local Authority may abate the nuisance itself i.e. by immobilising or removing alarms or other equipment, or even the car itself.

Another method of dealing with 'street nuisance' is to complain to your local Magistrates' Court. Remember to keep a record of all the incidents of noise etc. You must give the defendant at least 3 days' notice (for a complaint about noise) or 21 days' notice (in the case of other nuisances) in writing of your intention to take proceedings in the Magistrates Court. The Court will be able to give you information as to how to 'lay a complaint'. If the defendant is convicted the Court may impose a fine of up to £5000 and require him or her to take steps to prevent the nuisance occurring again. The Court may also order that the complainant's costs are paid by the defendant.

Appendices

Appendix 1

Checklist – what to do in the event of an accident

1 **Stop … stay calm!**
You are required by law to stop and remain at the site for a reasonable time to allow for details to be exchanged or given. **Failure to stop and/or exchange details is an offence**

2 **Call the emergency services if necessary**
– use your common sense!

3 **Exchange details with other parties** involved; details should include:

- ☐ Full name (and company name if a business vehicle)
- ☐ Full address
- ☐ Telephone numbers
- ☐ Other vehicle: Registration number
- ☐ Make and model
- ☐ Colour
- ☐ Date
- ☐ Time
- ☐ Location
- ☐ Weather conditions

4 Obtain names and addresses of witnesses.

5 Even if the police do not attend the scene of the accident you MUST report the accident if:

i)   someone other than you, the driver, was hurt;
ii) another vehicle or buildings or other property next to the road or street "furniture" (lamp post, bollard etc) was damaged;
iii) an animal was injured (though this does not include cats!).

You must report the accident to the police (a police constable or at a police station) at the earliest reasonably practicable time within the next 24 hours. **Failure to report is an offence.**

6 **Minor accidents**
Before things fade from your memory draw a plan of the accident and take photographs of the scene.

7 Report the Accident to your insurer even if you do not intend to make a claim: your policy may require it.

Appendix 2

Table of selected offences

	Where is it heard	Maximum sentence	Disqualification	Endorsement points	Other
Causing death by dangerous driving	Crown Court only	10 years' imprisonment and/or unlimited fine	Obligatory (minimum 2 years)	3-11	
Causing death by careless driving under the influence	Crown Court only	10 years' imprisonment and/or unlimited fine	Obligatory (minimum 2 years)	3-11	
Dangerous driving	Crown Court	2 years and/or unlimited fine	Obligatory (minimum 12 months)	3-11	
	or Magistrates	6 months and/or fine up to £5000	Obligatory (minimum 12 months)	3-11	
Careless or inconsiderate driving	Magistrates	Fine up to £5000	Discretionary	3-9	
Drink driving (being over the limit)	Magistrates	6 months and/or fine up to £5000	Obligatory (minimum 12 months)	3-11	
Driving – when unfit through drink/drugs	Magistrates	6 months or fine up to £5000	Obligatory (minimum 12 months)	3-11	
Being in charge when unfit through drink/drugs	Magistrates	3 months or fine up to £2,500	Discretionary	10	Can plead guilty by post
Refusing to take a breath test (roadside)	Magistrates	Fine up to £1000	Discretionary	4	
Refusing to give a specimen of breath, blood, or urine ('Driving')	Magistrates	6 months and/or fine of £1000	Obligatory (minimum 12 months)		
('Being in charge')	Magistrates	3 months and/or fine of £2500	Discretionary		
Driving whilst disqualified	Magistrates	6 months and/or fine up to £5000	Discretionary	6	
Using a car whilst uninsured	Magistrates	Fine up to £5000	Discretionary	6-8	Can plead guilty by post
Using a car without valid MOT	Magistrates	Fine up to £1000	—		Can plead guilty by post
Using a car without tax disc	Magistrates	Fine up to £1000 or 5 x tax amount	—		Can plead guilty by post
Speeding on a road	Magistrates	Fine up to £1000	Discretionary	3-6	Fixed Penalty Ticket. 3 pts + £40 fine
Speeding on motorway	Magistrates	Fine up to £2,500	Discretionary	3-6	Fixed Penalty Ticket. 3 pts + £40 fine
Failure to comply with a traffic sign	Endorsable: Magistrates	Fine up to £1000	Discretionary	3	Fixed Penalty 3 pts + £40
	Non-endorsable: Magistrates	Fine up to £1000	—		Fixed Penalty £20 fine

Appendix 3

Offences: failure to fulfil duties

Offence	Where is it tried	Maximum sentence	Disqualification	Endorsement points	Other
After Accident – failure to stop	Magistrates	6 months and/or fine up to £5000	Discretionary	5-10	
– failure to give details	Magistrates	6 months and/or fine up to £5000	Discretionary	5-10	
Failure to report on accident	Magistrates	6 months and/or fine up to £5000	Discretionary	5-10	
Failure to produce insurance certificate/MOT certificate	Magistrates	Fine up to £1000	—		Plead guilty by post
Failure to stop when required to by uniformed constable	Magistrates	Fine up to £1000			
Failure to give name or address where it is alleged you drove dangerously, carelessly or inconsiderately	Magistrates	Fine up to £1000			
Failure to produce driving licence when required	Magistrates	Fine up to £1000			

Appendix 4

Parking offences

Offence	Sentence	Fixed Penalty Ticket amount		Other
Parking on yellow lines	up to £1000	London Elsewhere	£30.00 £20.00	Towing away fee £105
Breach of regulations	up to £500	London Elsewhere	£30.00 £20.00	
Abuse of disabled parking spaces (on street)	up to £1000	London Elsewhere	£30.00 £20.00	
(off street)	up to £1000	Not applicable		
Failure to pay initial or excess charge	up to £500 + value of the parking charge	Not applicable		
Obstructing the Highway	up to £1000	London Elsewhere	£30.00 £20.00	Towing away fee £105

NB: All these offences are non-endorsable, i.e. no penalty points are endorsed on the driving licence.

Appendix 5

AA Road Rage Report

The following is a 1995 report by Matthew Joint, Assistant Head of Road Safety at the AA, on the concern over road rage incidents. It is reproduced here by kind permission of the AA.

WHAT IS 'ROAD RAGE'?

'Road rage' is a term that is believed to have originated in the US. In its broadest sense it can refer to any display of aggression by a driver. However, the term is often used to refer to the more extreme acts of aggression, such as a physical assault, that occur as a direct result of a disagreement between drivers.

The response to a stressful situation may often be anger. When we are confronted by a frustrating situation we often resort to aggression. This is often no more than verbal abuse. However, there are circumstances in which we may resort to physical violence. In the late 1980s, drivers in the US, apparently frustrated by increasing congestion, began fighting and shooting each other on a regular basis, victims of what the popular press termed 'road rage'. There is nothing to suggest that road rage is distinct from any other form of anger. But for many of us driving has become one of the most frustrating activities we are regularly engaged in. In the US, unverified figures of up to 1200 road rage related deaths a year have been reported. There is very little data available on the extent of the problem in the UK, although there have been increasing numbers of reports of violent disagreements between motorists over the last year.

In order to quantify the extent of the road rage problem The Automobile Association commissioned a survey of 526 motorists. The survey (carried out in January 1995) found that almost 90 per cent of motorists have experienced 'road rage' incidents during the last twelve months. 60 per cent admitted to losing their tempers behind the wheel.

Aggressive tailgating (62 per cent) was the most common form of "road rage", followed by headlight flashing (59 per cent), obscene gestures (48 per cent), deliberately obstructing other vehicles (21 per cent) and verbal abuse (16 per cent).

1 per cent of drivers claim to have been physically assaulted by other motorists.

Although 62 per cent of drivers were victimised by aggressive tailgaters, only 6 per cent confessed to doing it themselves. Gender differences were not as great as expected. 54 per cent of women admitted to aggressive driving behaviour (compared to 64 per cent of men).

Full details of the survey are given on page 96.

WHAT CAUSES 'ROAD RAGE'?

In some cases it appears that incidents of road rage are caused by simple misunderstandings between drivers. A driver may make a momentary error of judgement but the perception of another is that he is driving aggressively.

It is likely that the cause of the road rage extends beyond the immediate incident. An individual may have had a bad day at work or troubles at home. Often it may be difficult to tackle the cause of the frustration. It may therefore lie dormant, indeed the driver may not even identify feelings of frustration. However failure to indicate or a poor manoeuvre by another driver may be enough to trigger a release of the pent-up frustration which is directed towards the offending driver. In addition, there are a number of factors that explain why driving, in particular, should cause this frustration to manifest. Studies of animal behaviour have shown how rats and various primates can respond aggressively in response to overcrowding. It is reasonable to suggest that humans respond in a comparable manner.

Human beings are territorial. As individuals we have a personal space, or territory which evolved essentially as a defence mechanism – anyone who invades this territory is potentially an aggressor and the time it takes the aggressor to cross this territory enables the defender to prepare to fend off or avoid the attack. This may extend no further than a matter of a few feet or less. We may be prepared to reduce the size of this territory according to the available space (e.g. on a crowded tube train) but this can cause tension. In most cases if the territory is "invaded", if someone stands too close, our social education tends to result in defensive body language rather than physical aggression.

The car is an extension of this territory. Indeed, the territory extends for some distance beyond the vehicle, again providing room for the defender to prepare to fend off or avoid the attack. If a vehicle threatens this territory by cutting in, for example, the driver will probably carry out a defensive manoeuvre. This may be backed up by an attempt to re-establish territory – in spite of the rationalisations we used to account for our behaviour, flashing head lamps or a blast on the horn are, perhaps, most commonly used for this purpose. However, this may not always succeed in communicating the full depth of our feelings. As it is usually difficult to talk or even shout to the offending driver other non-verbal communication (offensive gesticulations) may be employed. Confrontations of this nature are not uncommon and are usually defused as the vehicles move away from each other. In some circumstances, the defending driver may wish to go one step further and assert his dominance. Many drivers admit to having chased after a driver to "teach him a lesson" often pressing him by moving to within inches of his rear bumper. This is comparable to the manner in which a defending animal will chase an attacker out of its territory. However, the result of such behaviour in drivers is, of course, potentially fatal.

Some of the worst cases of road rage have occurred where the opportunity for the vehicles to separate and go their own ways does not present itself. Gesticulations and aggressive manoeuvres have been exchanged in a rapidly degenerating discourse. Worked up into a rage one or both drivers have then got out of their vehicles and physically attacked their adversary and/or his vehicle.

Increasing levels of congestion on the roads have undoubtedly played a role in raising tempers among drivers and may partly explain why our survey revealed that the majority of motorists feel that the behaviour of drivers has changed for the worse in recent years.

Conflicts between drivers have also arisen because of unclear road priorities – where drivers have disagreed as to who has right of way, for example. In many cases the road priorities were determined at a time when the level of congestion and speed of traffic were considerably less than today.

Other drivers' failure to adhere to the rules of the road and ignoring signs e.g. where lanes merge or a lane is closed and drivers merge into the open lane at the last possible opportunity, is a commonly quoted cause of irritation among drivers. Improved means of law enforcement, perhaps with the aid of roadside cameras may reduce such transgressions.

Some psychologists have suggested that certain drivers are more susceptible to losing their tempers behind the wheel than others. The AA Foundation for Road Safety Research carried out a major study* designed to explore some of the lifestyle factors associated with drivers previously identified as 'safe' or 'unsafe' drivers. Although the AA Foundation study looked specifically at young male drivers it should be remembered that our recent survey found few age or gender differences in the prevalence of road rage.

The AA Foundation study revealed that one of the main factors influencing driver behaviour was mood. A greater number of unsafe drivers were affected by mood to a much larger extent than the safe drivers. It was suggested that this may be due to the fact that, for many of the unsafe drivers, the act of car driving is regarded as an expressive (rather than practical) activity. Being in a bad mood appears to have an adverse effect on driving behaviour and this effect appears to be most pronounced amongst unsafe drivers.

The AA Foundation study also found that unsafe drivers were more likely to be affected by the actions of other road users. Unsafe drivers were more likely to get wound up about (what they see) as inappropriate or 'stupid' actions of other road users. The bad moods of the driver were more likely to be exacerbated by other driver actions.

This evidence supports the view that some drivers are more likely to succumb to road rage. However, we should not conclude that this is a predisposition that cannot be altered. Drivers can adopt simple strategies that keep frustration, anger and rage in check.

HOW TO AVOID SUCCUMBING TO ROAD RAGE

Be aware of the precursors. Follow our general recommendations for avoiding stress and fatigue (see below). In particular, try to disassociate yourself from problems that have no bearing on the journey.

Never assume that an apparently aggressive act was intended as such. We all make mistakes. So don't bite back. If we take an example from studies of animal behaviour in the wild, the dominant animal in a group will rarely get involved in petty fights and disagreements. Although confident in his ability to defeat any opponent there is always the risk of injury.

Finally, draw reassurance from the fact that if you feel that someone is driving like an idiot every one else does.

HOW TO AVOID BECOMING A VICTIM

Our survey information indicates that the great majority of people (96 per cent) have not found that the road rage incidents have affected their confidence to drive. However, women and motorists aged 55-64 were the groups most likely to say that the last incident had affected their confidence. It must be stressed that the chances of any driver becoming the victim of a violent road rage attack are very small. The risks of driving alone can be exaggerated – be sensible about your safety but don't be

* 'Safe' and 'Unsafe' – a comparative study of younger male drivers
Authors: G Rolls and R Ingham from Department of Psychology from the University of Southampton

afraid to drive on your own. However, if you feel threatened by another motorist the following gives advice on how to defuse the situation or protect yourself:

If you're being hassled by another driver try not to react. Avoid making eye contact as this is often seen as confrontational. Don't be tempted to accelerate, brake or swerve suddenly – again, this may be seen as confrontational and increases your chances of losing control of your vehicle.

If a driver continues to hassle you or you think you are being followed, drive on to the nearest police station or busy place to get help.

In town, lock the car doors and keep the windows and sunroof only partly open.

When stopped in traffic, leave enough space to pull out from behind the car you are following.

If someone tries to get into your car, attract attention by sounding your horn or a personal alarm

Do not be tempted to 'have a go' and do not be tempted to carry any sort of 'weapon'. It may only provoke a potential assailant and could end up in his or her hands.

GENERAL ADVICE FOR REDUCING STRESS AND FATIGUE ON THE ROAD

Before starting a journey make sure that you know how to get to your destination and, if possible, have an alternative route in mind or at least an atlas in the car. Think about the timing of the journey – you wouldn't want to be travelling on the M25 at 5.15pm on a Friday.

Make sure your car is regularly serviced and carry out routine checks (tyre pressure, oil, water, etc.) regularly. Carry spares (bulbs, fan belt, emergency windscreen, etc.). Also, make sure that your windscreen is clean – particularly before a long journey. Peering through a dirty windscreen is a common source of stress and fatigue when driving. Also, have a window cloth, de-icer and sunglasses accessible.

Make sure that you are comfortable before starting the journey – adjust your seat and mirrors. If adjustable, you should also ensure that your seat belt and head restraint are correctly positioned.

Too often we have unreasonable expectations of journey times. Take journeys in easy stages and never remain behind the wheel of a car for more than three hours without a break. Don't try to cover more than 300 miles a day and, on a long trip, be careful on the second day of driving – this is when you tend to be most vulnerable to fatigue.

When you take a break make sure that you get out of the car, stretch your legs. Eat a light snack but avoid heavy meals, particularly at lunch time. Try to avoid eating in noisy, crowded places.

The likelihood of getting stressed while driving is largely dependent on your attitude of mind before you even turn the key in the ignition. Wind down before you crank up. Try to take one or two minutes to concentrate your mind on the task in hand and try to forget about other problems when driving.

Anticipate situations that are likely to wind you up and be tolerant of other road users' errors. If you find yourself in congestion try to accept that there is probably very little that you could have done or can do to prevent the delay.

Take remedial action before stress and fatigue get the better of you. Learn to spot the warning signs and develop positive coping strategies such as listening to the radio or a cassette (many people listen to novels or humorous tapes in jams).

Wind down the windows to increase ventilation and consciously breathe in the air slowly. Also, don't grip the steering wheel too hard as this will tense arm and neck muscles, leading to fatigue symptoms such as headaches.

If your mind is full of images of recent events or you are replaying conversations repeatedly in your mind make a conscious effort to slow them down until they become softer and more distant.

THE SURVEY IN DETAIL

The AA surveyed 526 drivers to establish the extent to which British motorists had experienced and perpetrated particular types of aggression when driving.

MAIN FINDINGS

Opinion of motorist behaviour

"Overall, how do you feel the behaviour of motorists has changed in recent years?"

The majority of motorists feel that the behaviour of drivers has changed for the worse in recent years. Motorists aged between 35-54 were most likely to feel this way (73 per cent), compared with those aged 55+ (62 per cent) and those aged under 35 (49 per cent).

All motorists	%
Better	2
Worse	62
No real change	34
Don't know	1

Receipt of particular types of aggressive behaviour

Motorists were then asked which of a list of particular types of behaviour they had experienced from other motorists in the last 12 months.

Almost nine in ten (88 per cent) of all respondents had experienced at least one of the types of behaviour listed above, in the last 12 months. Motorists aged 55+ were less likely to have done so (79 per cent).

All motorists	%
Aggressive tailgating (driving up very close behind)	62
Had lights flashed at me when other motorist annoyed	59
Received aggressive or rude gestures	48
Been deliberately obstructed or prevented from manoeuvring my vehicle	21
Received verbal abuse	16
Being physically assaulted	1
None of these	12

The majority of motorists had been tailgated (62 per cent) and had lights flashed at them by other motorists (59 per cent), and about half (48 per cent) had received aggressive or rude gestures. One in five had been deliberately obstructed, and fewer had received verbal abuse (16 per cent) or been physically assaulted by other motorists (one per cent)

Men were more likely than women to have received aggressive or rude gestures

(52 per cent and 42 per cent respectively), verbal abuse (19 per cent and 10 per cent respectively), and are more likely to have been deliberately obstructed (24 per cent and 17 per cent respectively).

Types of aggressive behaviour displayed towards other motorists

All respondents were then asked which types of behaviour they had done to other motorists.

60 per cent of all respondents admitted to doing one or more of the above to other motorists. It is debatable how willing people would be to admitting having done some of the more serious things described.

All motorists	%
Flashed lights at them when annoyed with other motorists	45
Given aggressive or rude gestures	22
Given verbal abuse	12
Aggressive tailgating (driving up very close behind)	6
Deliberately obstructed or prevented from manoeuvring my vehicle	5
Physically assaulted another motorist	*
None of these	40

Men were more likely than women to have done any of the things listed (64 per cent and 54 per cent respectively).

Similarly, motorists aged under 35 years old were most likely to admit to having done any of the things listed (76 per cent) than were those aged 35-54 years old (67 per cent) or those aged 55+ (34 per cent).

Almost half (45 per cent) of all motorists claimed, within the last 12 months, to have flashed their lights at another motorist when annoyed with them. One in five (22 per cent) have given aggressive or rude gestures, and one in ten (12 per cent) have given other motorists verbal abuse. Around one in twenty admit to having tailgated another driver (6 per cent) or deliberately obstructed another car (5 per cent). One respondent claimed to have physically assaulted another driver in the last 12 months.

Types of road on which the last incident was experienced

All respondents who had experienced an aggressive incident were asked on what type of road the last incident occurred.

All motorists	%
Main road	46
Motorway	26
Minor road	23
In a car park	4
Others	2

Almost half (46 per cent) last experienced one of these incidents on a main road. About a quarter mentioned a motorway (26 per cent) and a similar proportion said a minor road. One in twenty (4 per cent) incidents occurred in a car park.

Men were more likely to have experienced an incident on a motorway than were women (30 per cent and 18 per cent respectively). Similarly, older respondents aged 55+ were more likely to mention a motorway (34 per cent) than those aged 35-55 (23 per cent) or those aged under 35 years old (24 per cent).

Time of day at which the last incident was experienced

All those who had been victim of aggressive behaviour were asked whether it occurred after dark or during the day.

The majority (70 per cent) said the last incident occurred during the day, and 30 per cent said after dark. Younger motorists (aged under 35) were more likely to say after dark (44 per cent) than were 35-54 year old drivers (28 per cent) or motorists aged 55+ (15 per cent).

Extent to which aggressive behaviour affected your confidence when driving

All respondents having experienced any road rage incident were asked whether it affected their confidence when driving.

All motorists	%
Much less confident	1
A little less confident	3
Confidence not affected	96

Clearly, for the great majority of people (96 per cent), these incidents do not affect their confidence when driving. However, women (8 per cent) and motorists aged 55-64 (9 per cent) were the groups most likely to say that the last incident had affected their confidence when driving.

Index

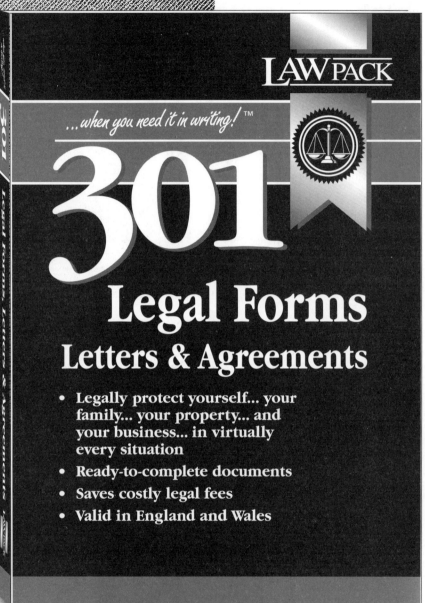

Law Pack *Do-It-Yourself* Guides

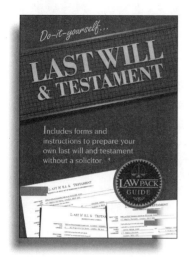

Last Will & Testament

With the help of this Guide writing a Will can be a straightforward matter. It takes the reader step-by-step through the process of drawing up a Will and provides helpful background information and advice. Will forms, completed examples and checklists are included.

Order no. B403
80 pages paperback £11.99
ISBN 1 898217 16 5

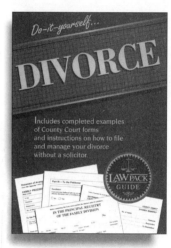

Divorce

File your own divorce and avoid expensive legal fees! This Guide explains the process from filing your petition to final decree. Even if there are complications such as young children or contested grounds this Guide will save you time and money.

Order no. B404
120 pages paperback £11.99
ISBN 1 898217 31 9

Small Claims

If you want to take action to recover a debt, resolve a contract dispute or make a personal injury claim, you can file your own small claim for under £3,000 without a solicitor. This Guide includes clear instructions and advice on how to handle your own case and enforce judgment.

Order no. B406
96 pages paperback £11.99
ISBN 1 898217 21 1

Limited Company

This Guide explains how to set up your own limited company without going to a solicitor. It is full of useful information and gives step-by-step guidance on the procedure. It also includes examples of Companies House forms, Memorandum and Articles of Association, resolutions and has answers to all questions.

Order no. B405
88 pages paperback £11.99
ISBN 1 898217 26 2

Employment Law

Whether you are an employer or an employee, you have rights in the workplace. This Guide is a comprehensive source of reference for anyone with questions about hiring, wages, employment contracts, termination, discrimination and other important issues. This essential guide puts at your fingertips all the important legal points employers and employees should know.

Order no. B408
134 pages paperback £11.99
ISBN 1 898217 46 7

Probate

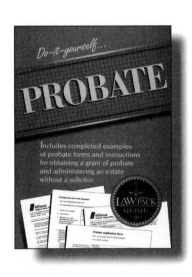

What happens when someone dies, with or without leaving a Will, and their estate needs to be dealt with? Probate is the process whereby the deceased's executors apply for authority to handle the deceased's assets. This Guide provides the information and instructions needed to obtain a grant of probate, or grant of letters of administration, and administer an estate without the expense of a solicitor.

Order no. B409
96 pages paperback £11.99
ISBN 1 898217 31 X

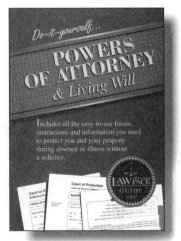

Powers of Attorney & Living Will

You never know when you might need someone to act on your behalf with full legal authority. What if you became seriously ill and needed business and personal interests looked after? This Law Pack Guide explains the difference between an Enduring Power Attorney (EPA) and a General Power of Attorney, and shows you how to create both. With the Living Will in this Guide you can also express your wishes regarding future medical treatment.

Order no. B410
76 pages paperback £11.99
ISBN 1 898217 62 9

- *Written and approved by lawyers*
- *Full instructions*
- *Valid in England and Wales*

Available in bookshops, stationers and office superstores.